*The French Stake in
Algeria, 1945–1962*

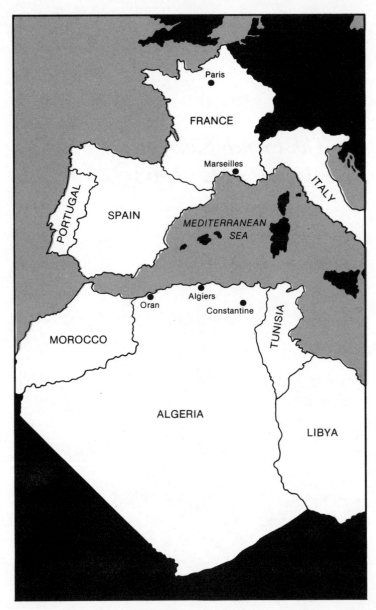

Algeria, France, and neighboring countries

The French Stake in
Algeria, 1945-1962

TONY SMITH

Cornell University Press

ITHACA AND LONDON

Cornell University Press gratefully acknowledges a grant from the Andrew W. Mellon Foundation that aided in bringing this book to publication.

First published 1978 by Cornell University Press.
Published in the United Kingdom by Cornell University Press Ltd., 2–4 Brook Street, London W1Y 1AA.

International Standard Book Number 0-8014-1125-4
Library of Congress Catalog Card Number 78-7713
Printed in the United States of America.
Librarians: Library of Congress cataloging information appears on the last page of the book.

To the memory of my parents

Contents

Preface

In retrospect, it is evident that the most important matter the French Fourth Republic had to face was the colonial problem. The debacle in Indochina, beginning within weeks of the regime's inauguration in the fall of 1946 and lasting until the summer of 1954, sapped the Republic's strength and provided the most glaring proof of its incompetence, while the duration of the struggle in Algeria that began on November 1, 1954, exhausted what remained of its legitimacy so that it quickly collapsed under the pressure of a military-settler uprising in Algiers in May 1958. It was not until the summer of 1962 that Charles de Gaulle's Fifth Republic could grant Algeria independence and so end the terrible trials of French decolonization. But if there are narratives aplenty on this sad chapter of French history, the efforts at interpretation remain relatively few. The task at this stage of the study of decolonization is to ask not simply what happened, but why it happened the way it did. There is an assumption here that history has a logic to its development and that the task of the social scientist is, in Henry James's words, to make clear "the figure in the carpet."

Sections of this book have appeared in journal articles over the last few years. A part of Chapter 4 was printed in somewhat different form under the title "Muslim Impoverishment in Colonial Algeria" in the Summer 1974 issue of the *Revue de l'Occident Musulman et de la Méditerranée*. A portion of Chapter 7 first ap-

peared as "The French Economic Stake in Colonial Algeria" in
French Historical Studies, Spring 1975. Sections of Chapters 2, 3, 6,
and 7 were adapted from "The French Colonial Consensus and
People's War, 1946–1958" in the *Journal of Contemporary History,*
October 1974. In each case, the editors have given their permission that the work be used here.

I would like to give particular thanks to Stanley Hoffmann and
the Center for European Studies, Harvard University, for financial support in the completion of this manuscript.

Finally, a word on nomenclature. I have used the word "colony" to denote any of a variety of French overseas possessions—
mandates, protectorates, and (in the case of Algeria) departments. And I have settled on the word "Muslim" to refer to the
Arab and Berber inhabitants of North Africa.

TONY SMITH

Tufts University
Medford, Massachusetts

Chronological Table
1944–1962

Year	Events in French Empire	Events in France	Events elsewhere
1944	Brazzaville Conference (Jan.) Ordinance on political rights in Algeria (March)	Liberation: DeGaulle leaves Algiers for Paris (Aug.)	Greek civil war begins (Nov.)
1945	Declaration Relative to Indochina (March) Sétif uprising (May) Vietnamese independence proclaimed (Sept.) Saigon coup (Sept.) Mandates over Syria and Lebanon ended	First Constituent Assembly elected (Oct.)	Yalta Conference (Feb.) German surrender (May) Japanese surrender (Sept.)
1946	Fontainebleau Conference (July) Bamako Congress of Black African leaders (Oct.) War begins in Vietnam (Nov.)	DeGaulle resigns (Jan.) Second Constituent Assembly elected (June) First legislature, Fourth Republic (Nov.)	Economic reconstruction of West Germany begins
1947	Madagascan uprising (March) DeGaulle's Declaration on Algeria (Aug.) Statute of Algeria (Sept.) Municipal elections, Algeria (Oct.) Vietnamese war one year old (Nov.)	Ramadier government formed (Jan.) Communists ousted from government (May)	Truman Doctrine (March) Marshall Plan (June) Independence for India, Pakistan, and Ceylon (Aug.)

Year	Events in French Empire	Events in France	Events elsewhere
1948	Tricked elections in Algeria begin (April) Vietnamese war two years old (Nov.)		Guerrilla war in Malaya Palestine/Israel independence Berlin Blockade (July) Disorders in the Gold Coast
1949	Vietnamese war three years old (Nov.)	National Assembly ratifies North Atlantic Treaty Organization (July)	North Atlantic Treaty Organization (NATO) created (April) First Soviet A-bomb (Sept.) Communist triumph in China (Oct.) Indonesian independence (Nov.)
1950	Tunis talks begin (June) Vietnamese war four years old (Nov.)		War in Korea begins (June)
1951	Vietnamese war five years old (Nov.)	Coal and Steel Community created (Dec.)	Mossadegh nationalizes Iranian oil
1952	Repression in Tunisia		Nasser to power in Egypt Mau-Mau uprising in Kenya
1953	Sultan of Morocco deposed (Aug.)		Stalin dies (Feb.) War in Korea ends (July)
1954	Geneva Conference on Indochina (July) Algerian revolution begins (Nov.)	Mendès-France government formed (June) European Defense Community (EDC) defeated (Aug.)	War in Malaya ends Southeast Asia Treaty Organization (SEATO) created by USA (Sept.)
1955	Soustelle named governor general in Algeria (Jan.) Tunis treaty ratified (July) Philippeville massacre (Aug.)	Faure government formed (Feb.)	Baghdad Pact formed Bandung Conference (April)

Year	Events in French Empire	Events in France	Events elsewhere
1956	Lacoste named resident minister in Algeria (Feb.) Moroccan independence Tunisian independence Framework law for French Africa voted (June)	Mollet government formed (Jan.) Mendès-France resigns Cabinet (May)	Suez invasion (Oct.) Hungarian invasion (Nov.)
1957	Framework law for Algeria defeated (Sept.)	Treaty of Rome creating the European Economic Community (EEC) ratified (July)	Ghanaian independence (March) Malaysian independence (Aug.)
1958	Framework law for Algeria voted (Feb.) Military-settler uprising in Algiers (May) Guinean independence (Sept.)	DeGaulle in power (June) Voters approve Fifth Republic (Sept.) Constantine Plan (Oct.) .	Anglo-American troops to Jordan and Lebanon (July)
1959			Castro to power in Cuba (Jan.) Riots in the Congo
1960	Black African states and Madagascar become independent (Dec.)	Revolt at the Barricades (Jan.)	Nigerian independence (Oct.) Congolese independence (June) Kennedy elected in USA (Nov.)
1961		Generals' revolt in Algiers (April) Secret Army Organization (OAS) officially launched (April)	Bay of Pigs invasion (April)
1962	Algerian independence (July)		

Abbreviations

AML, Association des Amis du Manifeste et de la Liberté
AOF, Federation of French West Africa (Afrique Occidentale
    Française)
EDC, European Defense Community
EEC, European Economic Community
ENA, Etoile Nord Africaine
FLN, National Liberation Front (Front de Libération Nationale)
GPRA, Provisional Government of the Algerian Republic (Gou-
    vernement Provisoire de la République Algérienne)
MNA, Mouvement National Algérien
MRP, Mouvement Républicain Populaire
MTLD, Mouvement pour le Triomphe des Libertés Démocratiques
NATO, North Atlantic Treaty Organization
OAS, Secret Army Organization (Organisation Armée Secrète)
OECD, Organization for Economic Cooperation and Development
OPEC, Organization of Petroleum Exporting Countries
PCA, Algerian Communist Party (Parti Communiste Algérien)
PCF, French Communist Party (Parti Communiste Français)
PDCI, Parti Démocratique du Côte d'Ivoire
RDA, Rassemblement Démocratique Africain
RPF, Rassemblement du Peuple Français
SAA, Syndicat Agricole Africain
SEATO, Southeast Asia Treaty Organization
SFIO, Parti Socialiste (Section Française de l'Internationale Ouvrière)
SIP, Sociétés Indigènes de Prévoyance
UDMA, Union Démocratique du Manifeste Algérien
UDSR, Union Démocratique et Socialiste de la Résistance

*The French Stake in
Algeria, 1945–1962*

Because of us, people of all races, hitherto for the most part plunged into a millenary torpor where history is not even written, discovered in their turn liberty, progress, justice. Because of us, new elites were born in these lands—whom we reared not that they would abuse others but that they would lead them toward a better and more worthy fate. . . .

To understand, one must see what has happened, one hundred years after its pacification, to our Algeria.

—Charles de Gaulle, May 15, 1945

Introduction

During the three decades since World War II, the most dynamic arena of international politics has not been the East-West confrontation, as so many anticipated, but the multitude of struggles between the "North," or industrial market states, and the "South," or preindustrial countries, struggles that go under the generic name of "decolonization." In the aftermath of the war, the networks of local groups that had everywhere formed the political backbone of European rule overseas—the native aristocracies, the ethnic minorities, the settler interests, the *comprador* merchants, the local *évolués*—either were overthrown or became transmuted into opponents of the foreign presence. In 1945, France ended her mandate over Syria and Lebanon. Then, in the summer of 1947, Great Britain recognized the independence of India, Pakistan, and Ceylon, thereby surrendering what for over a century and a half had been the greatest of the European imperial possessions. Within the space of twenty years, one-third of the peoples of the earth were freed of colonial rule. At the same time, millions of others who had been subject to Northern power without falling under formal colonial jurisdiction re-established their national identities. With the entry of the Chinese Communists into Peking in January 1949, the outlines of a new period of world history, one that signaled the end of the long era of unquestioned European hegemony over the preindustrial areas of the globe, seemed to be emerging from the ruins of the war.

Despite the speed of these developments and their local significance, such changes initially had only a limited impact on the overall structure of the international system, since they did not directly involve the key actor of the postwar order, the United States. To the contrary, by creating power vacuums in the late-developing world at the same time that it reduced the global importance of the European states, decolonization reinforced American hegemony. But within the last several years, two legacies of French and British imperialism to the postwar American order—Indochina and Israel—have been especially responsible for creating conditions that have severely shaken Washington's international position. For it was under the shadow of America's military defeat in Southeast Asia that the Organization of Petroleum Exporting States (OPEC) brought about the extraordinary rise in petroleum product prices which raised the value of OPEC exports from $29 billion in 1972 to over $130 billion in 1974.[1] The immediate result has been a strengthened offensive by the Southern states, associated in the Algerian-sponsored Group of 77, behind what Algeria's President Houari Boumédienne christened the "Program for a New International Economic Order." At the same time, these issues have created the possibility that the Northern states, grouped in the Organization for Economic Co-operation and Development (OECD) will fall out among themselves, divided as they are over a host of questions from access to raw materials to the protection of their investments in the South. The principal challenge to the American-dominated postwar order has come (at least to date, that is) not from the East, where it had so long been expected and whose relative power is continuing to grow, nor from America's economically dynamic friends, as some were beginning to speculate, but from those "night riders in black pajamas" (as Lyndon Johnson had called the Viet Cong)—the peoples of the Third World.[2]

These remarks should not suggest, however, that decolonization has been a unilinearly coherent historical phenomenon. The temptation is to try to simplify such a multiform process,

1. United Nations, *Monthly Bulletin of Statistics*, June 1975.
2. Tony Smith, "Changing Configurations of Power in North-South Relations since 1945," *International Organization*, Winter 1977.

either to force the particular case into what seems to be a general movement, or to assign unwarranted importance to a single historical factor. Certainly decolonization acquired an international momentum, and it is possible to isolate variables that appear to have had a marked influence on its progress regardless of time or place. But the various colonial areas were not dominoes responding to some inevitable "historical tidal wave of nationalism" any more than European governments had a set response to every colonial challenge whatever its nature. Nationalism in each case had its local pedigree. Different governments in Paris and London acted in noticeably different fashions. In this sense, there were multiple decolonizations, whose discontinuities, ambiguities, and uniquenesses must be respected, however much they may interfere with the desire to reduce history to a crystalline pattern, in the search for a single formula that puts order into its complexity.[3]

This book deals with a discrete moment of the general process of decolonization, the independence of Algeria from France. The primary question to be raised is why the French extraction from this part of North Africa proved so difficult. Why could not the Fourth Republic (1946–1958) arrange for Algerian independence despite the disastrous experience in Vietnam, despite the death toll in North Africa that was mounting into the hundreds of thousands, and despite the danger to the Republic itself that was increasing as right-wing elements, especially the army, were becoming more seditious? Or were these very occurrences somehow linked to the decision to stay sovereign in Algeria? What combination of interests and circumstances—economic, political, historical, and psychological—made it impossible for any leader or government of Fourth Republic France to put it as Charles de Gaulle did in 1961:

In the present world, at the period we are in, France has no interest in keeping dependent and under our law an Algeria which chooses another destiny; and France has no interest in carrying an Algeria population . . . which offers nothing in exchange for what it asks. . . . The reasons which formerly led certain civilized peoples to take under their direct control

3. Tony Smith, "A Comparative Study of French and British Decolonization," *Comparative Studies in Society and History*, January 1978.

certain others are in the process of disappearing, even in the minds of the former colonizers themselves. It now appears to the powerful that their future, their well-being, and the possibility of their world-wide action, depend on their own development and on cooperation with the former colonial countries, much more than on the domination of these peoples of other races. . . . It seems to me contrary to the present interest and new ambition of France to remain bound by charges and obligations which do not correspond to the requirements of her power and greatness.[4]

By the time of the outbreak of the revolution on November 1, 1954, Algeria had a population of nearly ten million, of whom some one million were of European origin, living for the most part in the coastal cities but possessing as well the best third of the country's arable land. The experience of 125 years of French rule had created of this area less than 500 miles south of Marseilles a colony unequalled in the empire in terms of trade, political bonds, and demonstrated strategic value. The actual size of the country—four times that of France—had only symbolic impor-tance, since most of it was mountain or desert waste, but Algeria was France's largest colonial trading partner, and the expectation of discovering significant reserves of gas and oil there (finally made in 1956 although anticipated since World War II) promised to increase handsomely its economic importance. In addition, the war had shown the strategic worth of these three North African departments (Algiers, Oran, and Constantine), when for a time Algiers had been the provisional capital of France and Algeria had been the main base of operations for the forces of Free France. Most important, perhaps, long before the difficult prob-lems of decolonization arose, the settler population had rooted itself in Paris and in the colonial bureaucracy in North Africa, obtaining repeated pledges from France that its rights would be protected. The importance of the area to France was therefore obvious, and it was to be expected that Paris would firmly counter any challenge to its sovereignty there, particularly when it came from nationalists as intransigent as those of the National Liber-ation Front (FLN), whose character made it improbable that France would continue to enjoy its many prerogatives in an inde-pendent Algeria.

4. Cited in André Passeron, ed., *De Gaulle parle* (Plon, Paris, 1962), pp. 287–290.

Yet, if these seem reasons enough for France to define her basic national interests in terms of maintaining control over Algeria, and hence are cause enough to explain the terrible trials of French decolonization, most commentators are in agreement that the process of granting independence to the overseas possessions was made especially difficult in the French case by the existence of a faulty system of government. According to this view (which Chapter 1 will present in some detail), the French might have fared much better had they possessed, like the British (or as de Gaulle proposed as early as 1945), a form of government which permitted leaders the kind of stability needed to formulate and to execute the intricate and delicate policies required for decolonization. Instead, the Fourth Republic institutionalized a system of government with a structure that so paralyzed its leaders that they could not deal with a problem the magnitude of decolonization, and especially with the loss of Algeria. On this point, socialist politicians, right-wing generals, and university analysts are for once in agreement.

It is the intention of this book, however, to argue that the most effective framework for understanding the French inability to decolonize easily is not one that looks to rational interests of an economic or strategic sort, nor one that places the onus on the shortcomings of a political system, but instead one that insists on a common perception or (following Emile Durkheim) a "collective conscience" of the French political elite in regard to colonial issues. The familiar proposition that in France an unworkable political system made a realistic colonial policy impossible will be set alongside an argument that reverses the chain of causation to maintain that it was rather an unrealistic policy, growing from what will be called the "colonial consensus," which upset and finally destroyed the Fourth Republic by dictating actions that again and again met with defeat. Admittedly, the French political system was a weak one whose divisions badly complicated the reaction to colonial nationalism. Yet, whatever the contribution of the system with its divisions was to the general debacle, its degree of responsibility was secondary to that of an instance of what, after de Gaulle, might be called "a certain idea of France," whose terms provided the basis for mobilizing the Republic for the empire's defense. That is, division within the system was not so serious that it prevented the formulation of a workable unity on colonial matters in general, and on Algeria in particular, which worked to exacerbate these conflicts. At certain critical moments the terms of this colonial consensus unambiguously appeared.

This proposition suggests that there were two aspects of the French difficulty and that they should be seen sequentially: consensus launched the Republic on a hopeless venture (Léon Blum and Paul Ramadier, both Socialists, with their Indochina policy in 1946–1947; Guy Mollet, another Socialist, with his Algerian policy in 1956–1957), only to splinter helplessly once the enterprise began to fail. Which of the two phases one concentrates on is therefore crucial. To date, the tendency has been to analyze the later period. The curious thing is that the evidence for the existence of a common mind on colonial issues seems so clear that the question arises of what obstacles prevented its earlier elucidation. There seems to be a tacit gentlemen's agreement to analyze only the later periods of colonial involvement, the paroxysms and paralysis which finally brought the Republic down. In this light no one was at fault: everyone looked on helplessly while an anonymous system somehow bungled into these disastrous wars. Apparently the experience is altogether too recent, too painful, and too embarrassing to men still in high position to recall the instances of pathetic self-deception, stubborn pride, and hypocrisy which at certain decisive moments were of common currency and which left their imprint clearly on the course of history. Contemporary accounts speak of governmental weakness, division, indecision, and immobilism. This account will try to right the balance by giving evidence of firmness, unity, decision, and resolve. Thus, to argue the significance of a determined consensus is not to reject the description of the Republic as structurally incompetent so much as to cast this incompetence in a new perspective.

For what marked these important periods of Socialist leadership—in 1946 and again in 1956—was not so much the fatal logic of a system as the fatal logic of a certain idea of France. Two comparisons illustrate this point. First, it is certainly striking that in 1946–1947, while the British Labour party was accelerating withdrawal from India in one of the most far-sighted colonial moves of this century, the French Socialists were sponsoring emotional demonstrations of support in the National Assembly for French soldiers in Indochina.[5] A second basis for comparison is provided by the difference between the French Socialist party (Section Française de l'Internationale Ouvrière [SFIO]) and the Parti Communiste Français (PCF) on colonial issues. Before the Cold War began in earnest (Communists were ejected from the government in Paris in May 1947) these two parties had developed significantly different positions on a variety of questions concerning the empire. Certainly, one may easily show that the Communists in 1945–1947 were not at all the militant anti-colonialists they had been in 1925–1927 at the time of the Rif War. But to make this point alone, as virtually a generation of non-Communist commentators have, is to ignore how much more liberal the PCF was on these matters than the SFIO. This is the case whether we look at the two parties' stands on a variety of issues including the Bamako Congress of Black African leaders in October 1946, the proposals for the Statute of Algeria in March 1947, or the repression in Madagascar in March 1947. Events ran true to form, then, when a Socialist governor general inaugurated fraudulent elections in Algeria in 1948, only to be protected by a Socialist interior minister and a silent Socialist party in the National Assembly. During Mollet's term as prime minister—the longest of the Fourth Republic—this policy was converted without hesitation from one of fraud to one of force. This is not to suggest, it should be emphasized, that the SFIO bore primary responsibility for the French posture on decolonization, but only to demonstrate how far left the colonial consensus reached.

For the Socialists shared with most of their fellow countrymen an image of France, a kind of collective conscience, born of the political paralysis of the thirties, the humiliation of the Occupation, the stern prophecies of de Gaulle, the fear of domestic communism, and the initial expectations and ensuing disappointments of the Resistance. With most of their fellow countrymen, they too experienced the loss of Indochina as the failure

5. Compare, for example, speeches by Prime Minister Attlee in March 1946 and March 1947 with those of Prime Minister Ramadier in March 1947, in Tony Smith, *The End of European Empire: Decolonization after World War II* (Heath, Lexington, 1975).

of a regime and feared that the decline of France to second-power status marked not so much an inevitable phase of world history, but the inner failing of a people. France had always used Algeria (like the rest of the empire) as the powerful do the weak, reckoning her a counter in interests Paris had elsewhere, able first to neglect, then to mythologize about her Muslim population. But increasingly after World War II, Algeria, like so many other areas under European rule, became something other than a voiceless pawn in the global calculations of Paris. That France could not accept this change had to do, certainly, with the real importance of her stake in North Africa and with the character of her regime. But it had to do as well with the terms of a colonial consensus which cast up an image of France that drove the Republic to its own destruction.

It was this common political language, with its generally recognizable symbols, values, hopes, and fears that gave the various definitions of the French stake in Algeria some sense of mutual identity. This is what made the Secret Army Organization (OAS), which in 1961 entered into a campaign of terror to prevent Algerian independence, first of all French and only quite secondarily "fascist." Can it be said that the military and settlers alone laid the revolution to foreign instigation? The Republic had officially denounced the unrepresentative character of the rebellion in the strongest terms and then, as if to show the sincerity of its words, sent the army to Suez. Had the military and settlers alone defined Algeria as vital to the national interest? A procession of political leaders had said no less and thereby made themselves the moral hostages of the military. Had the military and settlers alone found cause for the lengthening struggle not in the indigenous strength of the insurrection but in the shortcomings of the regime in Paris? Probably no belief was more commonly shared in France. Had the military and settlers alone confused the last hour of the empire with "the last chance" of France? Had not François Mitterrand, then interior minister, answered the Algerian uprising with the vision of what he called "African France"? "No task," he said, "is more beautiful nor more necessary for the work of our youth than to open this immense work-yard to our combined forces, across the space which extends from North to South, over 7,000 kilometers, across the metropole, across White Africa, across Black Africa."[6] Mitterrand spoke too of "Muslim France: . . . The seven million [*sic*] Muslim Algerians make France the second Muslim nation in the world (after Pakistan) [*sic*]. This we must not forget."[7]

Mitterrand's image was not new. Jean Jaurès, for one, had saluted the idea of "Muslim France" in 1912, just as de Gaulle had used the term in 1942.[8] Hence Jacques Soustelle's Jacobin credentials were quite in order when he, as ideological chief of the movement for French Algeria, declared that France needed spiritual *Lebensraum:* "France must have a 'Far West.' She has one: it is her 'Far South.' Instead of faint-heartedly closing herself in on her European territory in the pursuit of petty bourgeois comfort, she will draw from Africa a taste for wide-open spaces and hardy undertakings."[9]

No, the OAS was not representative of all colonial opinion, any more than the colonial consensus held in Paris was identical with the idea of France purveyed by the military-settler alliance. But there was a decided family resemblance.

The French stake in Algeria was at once economic, moral, strategic, and psychological. Each of these interests will come up in turn for consideration, but it is particularly the image or perception the French political elite had of their nation and the place of Algeria in relation to its future which this book singles out as the central factor holding France in North Africa. Certain aspects of this image were self-consciously formulated, but in important measure its strength, its power over French decision-makers, came from those of its terms that the leadership spontaneously assumed without question. Just as Thomas Kuhn speaks of the established presuppositions or paradigms which

6. *Journal officiel de la République française* (hereafter *Journal officiel*), *Débats parlémentaires, Assemblée Nationale: compte rendu in extenso des séances,* November 12, 1954, p. 4969.

7. Cited in *Paris-Presse,* December 12, 1954.

8. Charles de Gaulle, *Discours et messages: pendant la guerre, 1940–1946* (Plon, Paris, 1970), pp. 167–168; Jaurès cited in Georges Haupt and Madeleine Rebérioux, eds., *La Deuxième Internationale et l'orient* (Editions Cujas, Paris, 1967), pp. 151ff.

9. Jacques Soustelle, *Vingt-huit ans de Gaullisme* (La Table Ronde, Paris, 1968), pp. 287–288.

guide, but in unavoidable respects imprison, the thought of a scientific community, or as Susanne Langer writes of the central issues that dominate a period philosophically and thereby delineate a unified cultural era, so the French colonial consensus grew from the common experiences of a generation of Frenchmen who, whatever their differences, shared a generally compatible reading of the forces of contemporary history and drew similar conclusions for the role of France therein. Thus, after accounting for the rational economic, moral, and strategic interests of France in Algeria, and after making allowance for the deficiencies of the system of government under the Fourth Republic, the most important point has not been made. As the following pages will try to establish, the major stake the French had in Algeria was something more intangible: their sense of national identity.

While the terms of a national image develop out of the lived experiences of a people, they cannot be reduced simply to various socioeconomic indicators or historical events, but instead must be understood as a consensus actively produced by a group. A sensitive study of a certain climate of opinion or mood of the times will find words of established meaning, values of recognized worth, symbols of agreed-upon importance specific to the particular period in question. There may be commonly accepted ways of understanding the workings of history (for example, the fear of appeasement—the Munich reflex), or generally shared emotions born of historical experiences undergone together, which will set one generation off from another as surely as if they were peoples of different lands. Behind such collective images lies a complex of logical propositions on the ways of the world, a backlog of emotional concerns, and certain value preferences on how future history should look. Such constructs—a group's *Zeitgeist*—need not be totally coherent, least of all rational. Their peculiar logic will be a sort of "psycho-logic." Even though this logic be understood as the product of experiences lived, these constructs are ultimately comprehensible only within the terms of their own unique frames of reference. Since the collective conscience which holds the image of the group is, as in religion, the group's own common invention, it is irreducible historical data. So the past and the future coexist with the present which itself must be grasped not as a frozen moment, but as a point where political actors are speaking in the idiom of other periods. The convolutions of this process have a structural integrity that defies reduction to social and economic categories, however much these may be indispensable in understanding the origin and terms of the image. The historian may, then, analyze the French reaction to the Algerian revolution as a psychologist might approach his subjects' interpretations in a thematic aperception test. In this sense, Algeria constituted a sort of historic inkblot where Frenchmen, in purporting to account for events there, instead revealed much more of the political lessons, hopes, and fears they had acquired from other experiences and had projected onto Algeria in disregard of the objective circumstances there. It is not necessary to claim that this is the only way history should be studied in order to maintain that such an approach should be integral to social analysis.[10]

On the other hand, such collective consciences can never be analyzed apart from their roots in experience. It is a certain group at a given moment that establishes a cognitive account of its situation and so decides its behavior. If a group's collective conscience or *Geist* cannot be reduced to social structure, neither can it be understood apart from it. In short, perception cannot be understood apart from history any better than history can be understood apart from men's intentions in acting. To abandon either terms of the process—consciousness or situation—is, except for heuristic reasons, to reify history either into an act of mind (idealism) or into the movement of vast impersonal forces (positivism). So, in the case of the process of French decolonization, it is important to understand how the French came to see

10. Many social psychologists hold to this view although it is seldom self-consciously applied by historians. Its methodological defense may be found in Emile Durkheim, *The Elementary Forms of Religious Life* and *The Rules of Sociological Method* as well as in Jean-Paul Sartre's *Search for a Method* (the introductory section of *Critique de la raison dialectique*). For works by Americans, see Kenneth Boulding, *The Image;* Peter Berger and Thomas Luckmann, *The Social Construction of Reality;* and Robert Jervis, "Hypotheses on Misperception," *World Politics,* April 1968. While used by many historians, this approach usually receives no more systematic elaboration than that given it by John Gallagher and Ronald Robinson in *Africa and the Victorians.* I have used this method on one of its chief theoreticians in "Idealism and People's War: Sartre on Algeria," *Political Theory,* I (November 1973).

their place in the postwar world. Rational calculations and genuine insights, not to speak of the effect of domestic political struggles, clearly shaped their policy. But other perceptions were key as well—those of the evolving structure of the postwar world, of the character of nationalist uprisings in Indochina and Algeria, and of the French themselves—which tended to distort reality and which proved extremely difficult to correct.

Political analysis typically favors the study of interests over images (assuming, not without reason, that the former usually dictates the latter) and in the domain of the image tends to favor the rational (for example, class consciousness or balance of power considerations) over the nonrational. But what must often be explained is how *perceived* interests may run counter to *objective* interests, indeed how frequently men follow their perceptions to the destruction of their interests. The stake in politics, it is often safe to say, is not interest but image. As Freud put it in 1916: "It would seem that nations still obey their immediate passions far more readily than their interests. Their interests serve them, at most, as rationalizations for their passions; they parade their interests as their justification for satisfying their passions."[11]

11. Sigmund Freud, "Reflections on War and Death," 1916.

1 The Case against the Importance of a Consensus

Twenty years after the collapse of the Fourth Republic, it is apparent that despite the regime's many successes, most notably perhaps in the economic field, its failure to deal at all adequately with the colonial problem brought about its fall. The war in Indochina, beginning only weeks after the inauguration of the Republic in the fall of 1946, lasted nearly eight years, to be followed less than four months after its termination by the outbreak on November 1, 1954, of revolution in Algeria. Forty months later, its legitimacy exhausted, the Republic fell to a military-settler uprising in Algiers, and de Gaulle's Fifth Republic (confirmed by the referendum of September 28, 1958) came to power.

In response to the question of *why* the process of decolonization was so difficult, the most general response has been to point to the manifold structural shortcomings of the governmental system under the Fourth Republic (pejoratively referred to as *le système*). Perhaps the most scathing comment on the Republic's debility was made by de Gaulle during a press conference in October 1948. Asked by a journalist, "Mon Général, . . . if you return to power will you significantly modify the foreign policy of France?" de Gaulle bitingly replied: "I will not have to change the foreign policy of France since at present France has no foreign policy. Her regime does not permit it, any more than it permits her to have an economic policy worthy of the name, a social policy, or a financial policy, etc. The truth is, there is nothing. Thus, I will not change this policy which does not exist, but I will make the policy of France."[1]

Nearly a decade later, on May 15, 1958, when this seemingly oracular leader moved to replace the Fourth Republic, he confirmed the justice of his earlier warning by pointing out the obvious consequences of a deficient public authority: "The degradation of the State inevitably brings the estrangement of the associated peoples [colonials], trouble within the fighting army, national dislocation, and the loss of independence. For twelve years, confronted by problems too stubborn for a regime of parties, France has been engaged in this disastrous process."[2]

Amended in various fashions, de Gaulle's judgment is shared by many others, to such an extent that a general consensus seems to exist among scholars, military officers, politicians, and indeed, the public at large: the governments of the French Fourth Republic were simply too weak to make clear, far-sighted policy and then to implement it. The tragic throes of decolonization were a direct consequence.

The colonial problems of the forties and fifties were not the only matters where ineffective and unstable governments had meant setbacks, even disaster, for France. This had been the experience as well of what Stanley Hoffmann has called the "stalemate society"—the Third Republic (1871–1940)—which, like the Fourth, collapsed under the pressure of international events it had done little to forestall and, indeed, had exacerbated by its very incapacity. As cabinet crises succeeded one another, as public indifference and hostility toward the regime mounted, and as in one domain after another the absence of clear, able policy was evident, it came to seem that the Fourth Republic was the reincarnation of the Third.

But to tell us the system was weak does not explain why. Philip Williams, perhaps the leading British analyst of French domestic politics, ascribes the National Assembly's incompetence to its multiple divisions which, in turn, he traces outside the parliament

1. Charles de Gaulle, *La France sera la France* (Bouchy et Fils, Paris, 1951), p. 153.
2. *L'Année politique, économique, sociale et diplomatique,* 1958 (Presses Universitaires de France, Paris, 1959), p. 534.

to the historical development of the French economic and social structures:

[In France] three issues were fought out simultaneously: the eighteenth-century conflict between rationalism and Catholicism, the nineteenth-century struggles of democracy against authoritarian government, and the twentieth-century dispute between employer and employed. . . . Since politics turned on several different conflicts instead of one, there was a coherent majority neither in the country for a single party nor in the Parliament for a lasting coalition. Associates on one issue were bitter opponents on others. MRP [Mouvement Républicain Populaire], for example, worked with Socialists and Radicals, and most Conservatives in defending the regime against Communists and Gaullists. On matters involving working-class interests and sometimes on colonial questions, it sympathized with the Socialists and Communists; Radicals, Conservatives and (until 1951) RPF [Rassemblement du Peuple Français] were hostile to its views. But over church schools MRP found its friends (or competitors) among Gaullists and Conservatives, while all Socialists and most Radicals joined with the Communists against it. And on Europe it agreed with most Conservatives and Socialists and opposed Communists and RPF, with the Radicals split. So complicated a situation put a high premium on the art of maneuver and facilitated other, temporary combinations. Electoral tactics united MRP with Communists against all other parties in defense of proportional representation; Socialists and RPF often held similar views on the problem of Germany.[3]

Here, then, the sociologist's idea of "cross-cutting" cleavages works to explain governmental weakness. Although such cleavages are generally considered a source of political stability when present in the population at large (since they tend to assure all citizens some identity of interest with one another and hence some common stake in government), the same cleavages reflected too faithfully within the structure peculiar to the French ruling body resulted in constant compromise and change, blocking the establishment of long-term policies.

This problem of political factionalization was aggravated by a form of voting that encouraged multiple parties and by the recurrent "disloyal" opposition on the part of the Communist party and various groups on the right that at times worked for the collapse of the Republic altogether. Lack of consensus on what constituted legitimate rule meant that the system of government

3. Philip Williams, *Crisis and Compromise: Politics in the Fourth Republic* (Anchor, New York, 1966), pp. 3, 32.

itself was not neutral, that it did not constitute "an agreed-upon platform from which to disagree." Thus, to maintain a third-force government in the immediate postwar years in the face of both Communist and Gaullist opposition, those in power had to avoid serious conflict among themselves. This could work only if, on the one hand, they avoided insisting too strongly on their own programs yet, on the other, gave in when their partners in power proved intransigent in theirs.[4]

Nor within the parliament was there a process whereby these centrifugal forces could be held together. Nicholas Wahl suggests that the problem might have been less critical had a method existed of integrating popular representation with executive competence,[5] for a fragmented political authority had first prevented the concentration of effort behind a single policy, then sheltered the members of government from the storm of criticism set loose by inaction. In this sense, the problem had a self-perpetuating logic: diffused responsibility was both a cause of governmental ineffectiveness and a refuge from it. Nathan Leites has described this process as a "game" whose most outstanding characteristic was "passing the buck."[6] The presidential office of the Fifth Republic was hoped by many to be the answer to this structural defect.

Michel Crozier and Stanley Hoffmann argue still another cause of the weakness of French government in their discussion of general French attitudes toward authority. They note that long before the Revolution of 1789 the French had lived under a strong central authority, that this tradition had been maintained as much by the Republicans with their "one and indivisible nation" as by the two Napoleons, and that the French had acquired certain habits in regard to strong central authority as a result. In a word, these were practices making central power necessary but also tending to make it weak, for though French groups resisted encroachment on their prerogatives, they nonetheless depended

4. See, for example, Raymond Aron, *Immuable et changeante: de la IVè à la Vè République* (Calmann-Lévy, Paris, 1959), *passim.*

5. Nicholas Wahl, "The French Political System," in Samuel Beer and Adam Ulam, eds., *Patterns of Government* (Random House, New York, 1962).

6. Nathan Leites, *On the Game of Politics in France* (Stanford University Press, Stanford, 1959). See also Alfred Grosser, *La IVè République et sa politique extérieure* (Armand Colin, Paris, 1967), p. 51.

on a higher authority to resolve their most difficult problems. Contemporary manifestations of this long-standing attitude have been studied in the office, the factory, and the classroom as well as in political life.[7] We can, then, extrapolate from this that jealous resentment of strong leaders could be expected within the National Assembly as the career of one of its most outstanding members, Pierre Mendès-France, suggests. Quarreling politicans had finally referred the Indochinese problem to him, only to topple him some months thereafter, partly in response to his very success. Not surprisingly, Mendès-France laid the blame for weak French government on the mediocre politicans charged with running *le système:*

Their method has become classic: if the truth is hard, if it takes some courage to speak it, then, in order not to lose popularity, they begin by varnishing it, if not covering it with, of course, the intention to act so that it gradually becomes evident. . . . This game of hide-and-seek with the truth is the fundamental cause of our disappointments of these past years, the direct cause of the failure of the Fourth Republic.[8]

Nor, finally, should one forget that weakness is a relative term when measuring a government against the problems to be solved. Alfred Grosser stresses the manner in which the enormity of the issues involved contributed to division, and thereby to weakness, within the political body:

France had at once the corrosive and exalting privilege to be the microcosm of world politics, to be torn by the two conflicts which dominated the world in the middle of the twentieth century. The opposition between the Communists and the diverse anti-Communists was only sketched out in January 1946. It assumed its true dimension only in 1947. The confrontation between the old states and the young nationalisms was perceptible during the war. It continued to grow more violent for reasons which for the most part had nothing to do with French politics. Almost all Frenchmen claim to be liberals. But this double cleavage rendered a fully liberal policy about impossible: in order to give liberty to the colonial peoples, there was no majority but with the Communists; in order to defend the liberties that the Communists would

7. Michel Crozier, *The Bureaucratic Phenomenon* (University of Chicago Press, Chicago, 1964); Stanley Hoffman, "Protest in Modern France," in Morton Kaplan, ed., *The Revolution in World Politics* (Grove Press, New York, 1962).

8. Pierre Mendès-France, *Gouverner c'est choisir, III: la politique et la vérité* (Juilliard, Paris, 1958), pp. viii, xi.

destroy, there was no majority except with those who refused them in Africa and Asia. Italy without colonies and Great Britain without a Communist electorate were better divided.[9]

No other statement is so generally cited by writers seeking a capsule formula to explain the difficulties of French decolonization than this judgment by Grosser.

In regard to the postwar problems of empire, then, it is no surprise that nearly every commentator singles out what is variously called "immobilism," "lack of clear goals," "absence of a policy," "delay and indecision," or "division and hesitation" as characteristic of the Fourth Republic. Raymond Aron insists it was less decision than indecision which spiraled into the war in Indochina.[10] Jean Barale writes that "the policy of the Fourth Republic in regard to war lacked not only greatness and force, but still more, sureness and unity. The Fourth Republic never could decide either to win the war or to put an end to the hostilities."[11] The scandals of the *affaire des généraux,* the *affaire des fuites,* and the *affaire des piastres* were only the surface manifestations of a venality and an ineptness infecting the French system of government root and branch. Observers quote approvingly General Henri Navarre who, though admitting the military error lying behind his defeat at Dien Bien Phu, nonetheless insisted on a more important reason for catastrophe:

The first reason from which almost all the others flow is the absence of a policy. From the first to the last, our leaders never dared tell the country that there was a war in Indochina. They were never able to get the country into the war nor to make peace. They were unable to define a line of conduct and to impose it on those who represented France on the spot. . . . The evasions, mistakes, cowardices built up over eight years are too numerous and too continuous to be imputed to the men, or even to the governments, which succeeded each other in power. They are the fruits of a regime. They proceed from the very nature of the French political system.[12]

9. Grosser, *La IVè République,* p. 398.
10. Aron, *Immuable et changeante,* p. 137.
11. Jean Barale, *La Constitution de la IVè République à l'épreuve de la guerre* (Librairie Générale de Droit et de Jurisprudence, Paris, 1963), p. 23 (see also pp. 199, 337).
12. Navarre's words are frequently cited. See, among others, Grosser, *La IVè République,* pp. 285–286; and Raoul Girardet, *La Crise militaire française, 1945–1962* (Cahiers de la Foundation Nationale des Sciences Politiques, number 123, Paris, 1964), p. 163n.

Moreover, debility at the center fed insubordination on the periphery. As Robert Schuman put it in a much-cited article in 1953, "The *fait accompli* is a great and constant temptation to which resident generals have merit when they resist, to the extent they do not succumb to it. Moreover, they themselves are in an analogous position in relation to certain groups (police, secret service, etc.)"[13]

As with Indochina, so with Algeria. With what might be called a fatalistic feeling of inevitability concerning the ultimate outcome, the Fourth Republic faced the insurrection in North Africa, determined at once that the area would remain French, yet fearful it well might be lost, not because of the nationalist determination of the rebels but because of the inner bankruptcy of the regime. Here once again were the succession of cabinet crises, the debilitating government debates, the prolongation of the fighting, and the apparent absence of an overall policy coordinating political, diplomatic, and military moves. At the root of the colonial disaster lay the French system of government.

Yet, neither separately nor taken together are these explanations for the failure of the French to decolonize more easily satisfactory. Since such explanations all assume a regime incapable of policy formulation in postwar France, any idea that a common mind on colonial matters was held by the French political elite would naturally be dismissed out of hand. Even less agreement would exist that such a common mind could deal systematically, with resolve and perseverance, on issues raised by colonial nationalism. But suppose it were possible to demonstrate the existence of an implicit policy, to be called the colonial consensus, to which the leaders of the Republic would hold tenaciously and whose very inflexibility would make the survival of the political system unlikely? Then it would be legitimate to speculate that it was not so much the system that was at fault—as is generally alleged from de Gaulle's first warnings until the present day—as the persistence of this consensus, the logic of which fixed the Republic on a self-destructive course.

While I intend to support this contention with a review of the Fourth Republic's policy, briefly in regard to Indochina and in

13. Robert Schuman, *La Nef*, March 1953, cited in Grosser, *La IVè République*, p. 52.

more detail with respect to Algeria, the long struggle over the "framework law" of 1957 proposing to restructure Algeria politically serves as a capsule illustration. As in 1947, when the National Assembly voted the Statute of Algeria, the French were deliberating what the British might call Home Rule, that is, a special political arrangement for Algeria giving the Muslim population a larger voice in local affairs as well as according them certain reforms designed to recognize their distinct "personality." With the political parties split internally as well as among themselves, with divisions within both the Cabinet and the Assembly's Interior Commission (which was to review the bill), and with disagreement between the Commission and the conclusions finally reached by the parties working in their "round table" meetings, no single measure involving Algeria seems at first inspection more indicative of the profound disunity among the political leaders of France nor gives more evidence of governmental paralysis. As William Andrews, for one, put it, the Republic had "descended deeper and deeper into a pit of weakness, indecision and complacent despair . . . its dance of death had reached phrenetic tempo."[14] In February 1958, the bill finally passed the Assembly, but only after three months of debate and the fall of the Maurice Bourgès-Maunoury government on one of its readings.

Yet, from the perspective of the present study, surely the most striking aspect of the bill was *not* the intensity of the debate surrounding it, but the fact that a proposal of this nature, contemplating as it did alternative ways of keeping Algeria French, could be discussed at all nearly three years after the outbreak of the revolution. There is no need to dig deeply into the labyrinthine complexities surrounding the final rendition of the bill other than to suggest the common bonds of hope and illusion which held together the apparently divided deputies. Prime Minister Edgar Faure had suggested some new arrangement in 1955, and in 1956 Prime Minister Mollet had given more body to the notion with a blueprint calling for the effective Balkanization of Algeria. As it was eventually presented to the Assembly by Prime

14. William Andrews, *French Politics and Algeria* (Merideth, New York, 1962), p. 90 (and see Chapter 7 entire).

Minister Bourgès-Maunoury in the fall of 1957, and finally passed by the government of Félix Gaillard early in 1958, the bill underwent additional modifications. However, all of these formulations accepted the idea of dividing Algeria into several autonomous territories, each with its own assembly elected by universal suffrage (although the Europeans would predominate around Algiers and Oran). Furthermore, all accepted the notion of some form of federative body uniting these disparate assemblies while agreeing that the great bulk of political power would remain firmly in the hands of Paris and its appointed representatives in Algeria. Article 14 of the bill as voted enumerated the powers specifically reserved to Paris: "citizenship and French civil law; foreign affairs, Algerian defense, [military] recruitment, general security; institutional organization of Algeria; . . . electoral system; currency, exchange, treasury, customs, taxes, public expenditures; public education, public domain energy."[15]

For a time there had indeed been a provision in an earlier version of the bill permitting Paris to transfer certain of these reserved powers to the federal Algerian assembly. But despite the brave assurances of Socialist leader Mollet that his group stood for a liberally conceived measure ("Let no one count on us to backtrack on the key proposals of the bill and its framework"[16]), his party ultimately agreed to delete this provision. It also voted for the creation of secondary bodies under effective settler control to be placed alongside the proposed Algerian territorial assemblies and to have de facto veto power over these assemblies' deliberations.

In the minds of the politicians, the bill's primary purpose was to convince the Muslim population that the French government meant to commence serious reforms which would meet their legitimate demands for more control over their own affairs. In the language of the times, the bill was to be a "psychological shock," rallying the Muslims from their supposed hesitation between the French and the FLN, letting them turn with "renewed

15. For the French text, see Thomas Oppermann, *Le Problème algérien: données historiques, juridiques, politiques* (Maspero, Paris, 1961), pp. 299ff. For earlier formulations, see *Le Figaro*, September 23, 1957; *Le Monde*, September 20, 1957; and *Perspectives*, September 28, 1957.

16. *Le Monde*, September 20, 1957.

confidence" toward the authority of Paris. To the extent that the
bill generated a shock, however, it worked on an unintended
group: the settlers. The words of Baretaud, president of the
mayors of the department of Algiers, in attacking the measure
summed up this mood: "The Muslims in the countryside care
very little about the bill. The same is true for the large majority of
the urban population. . . . On the other hand, for the European
of the countryside or the city, this is a plan of abandonment. The
softness of some and the cowardice of others exasperate them
and they are ready to take extreme measures."[17]

Similarly, certain patriotic associations in Algeria wrote to President René Coty: "For two months the French of Algeria . . . have
been seeing with astonishment their future being played out in
confusion, intrigues, and deals."[18] Indeed, toward the end of
August 1957, a number of groups in Algeria—students, teachers,
veterans, and various political organizations—had begun to plan
a mammoth strike and demonstration, set for September 18, in
protest against this new act of metropolitan interference. Only
forceful statements by Resident Minister Robert Lacoste and
General Jacques Massu, both greatly respected in the settler community, managed to avert the action. Eight months later these
men would refrain from issuing their restraining orders, and the
Fourth Republic would fall at the end of a movement initiated by
mob action in Algiers.

The question then obviously arises: Was there a failure to
arrive at a realistic colonial policy because of the debilitating
system of French government, as is generally supposed, or was it
instead a certain colonial consensus whose persistence proved
fatal to the Republic? The latter seems the more appropriate
conclusion. How else can we understand the *active* role the leaders
of France took in the downfall of their own regime, the impetus
behind the allocation of wealth, manpower, and passion required
to keep an army of 500,000 men (plus Muslim auxiliaries) in
Algeria? When Barale, for example, speaks in the work cited
earlier of *la guerre* as though it were an evil demon come from
afar, clamping itself onto an unsuspecting Assembly and by its

17. *Le Monde,* September 25, 1957.
18. *Le Monde,* September 26, 1957.

own power bleeding this body powerless, he gives us no indication of French initiative, determination, and responsibility in the genesis of the wars in Indochina and Algeria. "Indecision," "immobilism," "division?" Certainly these were not the hallmarks of two key Socialist governments, those of Ramadier and Mollet.

Nor is Grosser correct when he, like so many others, argues that "but for the Communists," majority opinion would somehow have dealt more easily with decolonization. This assumes a will to decolonize on the part of the non-Communist left which, aside from scattered groups and individuals, there is precious little evidence to substantiate. To the contrary, it was the PCF, alone of the major parties in France, which respected the historical limits of the moment and recognized early the kind of flexibility a successful postwar imperial policy must possess. Thus, while the Communist party tended to discourage independence movements in the empire, it chose to work with rather than repress them, seeking to ensure that, should separation become unavoidable, it would occur under the auspices of a nationalist elite best able to represent the local population and preserve the area from the encroachment of foreign powers (especially the United States). In most respects, the PCF compares well with the Labourites. To imply as Grosser does, in an analysis far too easily accepted by many, that the non-Communist left would have worked with the Communists toward a liberal colonial policy simply denies the evidence. What sort of liberal schemes were Paul Ramadier and Marius Moutet unable to realize toward Algeria, Indochina, or Madagascar because of their inability to work with the PCF in 1946–1947? How were Jules Moch and Marcel-Edmond Naegelen in their actions in Algeria, or Paul Béchard and Laurent Péchoux with their policies in West Africa in 1948 thwarted in their liberal designs by their distance from the Communists?

To read these analyses is to believe that France bungled into fifteen years of colonial warfare, that an anonymous system worked its own mechanical destruction free of responsible human agency. It is as though there were a concerted effort to whitewash the men and parties of the period rather than admit the shortcomings of the colonial consensus. But how are we otherwise to make sense of Socialist Prime Minister Mollet's ringing declaration made *after fifteen months* in office?

The government has never ceased to give absolute priority to the necessities of Algeria. It has never hesitated before measures which might have
appeared very unpopular. . . . On the military level, the government
intends to leave no doubt about its decision to continue to send regularly
the draft army to complete a part of its time in Algeria, even, and I should
say especially, when calm shall have been re-established. . . . Let us then
reaffirm the essential and demonstrate a unanimous will that France
remain present in Algeria.[19]

Mollet was, in fact, quite accurate in this estimation of his
government's material and moral dedication to the preservation
of French Algeria. Yet when the Fourth Republic fell, Mollet
joined with the others in blaming not his own policy but the
shortcomings of the political system for French reversals abroad.
By his account, the regime "was undermined from within by its
own contradictions. The mutual neutralization of the parties
provoked a sort of internal paralysis."[20] As we have seen, most
other commentators agree with him and so exonerate his policy
for the responsibility it should bear.[21]

The aim of the following pages is to establish the essential terms
of the colonial consensus, to explain its genesis in the life of the
Third Republic and in the experiences of World War II, and to
account for its persistence from its inception in the winter of 1945
until the collapse of the Republic in the spring of 1958.

19. *Journal officiel,* March 27, 1957, pp. 1906, 1909; for excerpts from the
speech see Smith, *End of Empire,* pp. 128–131.
20. Guy Mollet, *13 mai 1958–13 mai 1962* (Plon, Paris, 1962), p. 1.
21. A partial exception to this generalization is D. Bruce Marshall, *The French
Colonial Myth and Constitution Making in the Fourth Republic* (Yale University Press,
New Haven, 1973). Marshall says of "the colonial myth" that its "vision dominated
the French approach to decolonization in the postwar period, preventing French
leaders from realistically assessing the dimensions of native nationalism and
predisposing them to respond to nationalist demands in ways that made it impossible to avoid the tragic colonial wars that later destroyed the Republic" (p. 2).
Marshall, however, dates the breakdown of the myth in the fall of 1946 (see his
Introduction and Chapter 9, "The Decline of the Colonial Myth").

2 The Origins of the Colonial Consensus

In his first radio broadcast to the people of Occupied France, in the blackest hour of the nation's history, Charles de Gaulle sought to rally his country with the hope of empire: "But has the last word been said? Must hope disappear? Is our defeat final? No! . . . For France is not alone! She is not alone! She has behind her a vast empire."[1] And again, on June 18, 1942: "There is one element which, in these terrible trials, has revealed itself to the nation as essential to its future and necessary to its greatness. This element is the empire. First of all because it is in the empire that the base for our recovery was constituted."[2]

In fact, however, the empire had not answered de Gaulle's appeal with much alacrity. Félix Eboué, governor of Chad, had managed to rally French Equatorial Africa behind de Gaulle, but elsewhere the empire remained loyal to the Vichy government, despite attacks by Free French forces at Dakar and in Syria.[3] Ultimately the Allied landing in North Africa in November 1942 persuaded the other African territories to gather behind de Gaulle's banner, so that the French forces which later invaded Italy and moved into France from the south were for the most part composed of colonial soldiers. As de Gaulle reminded his countrymen at one of the first meetings of the Provisional Assem-

1. Charles de Gaulle, *Pendant la guerre*, p. 3.
2. De Gaulle, *La France sera la France*, p. 161.
3. Brian Weinstein, *Eboué* (Oxford University Press, New York, 1972).

bly in liberated Paris: "Can one imagine what the outcome of the conflict might have been had the German forces been able to use the French territories in Africa? To the contrary, how important was our North Africa as the base of departure for the liberation of Europe."[4]

It followed, then, almost as a matter of course, that after the war, France would preserve her empire. In time of peace it assured her greatness, in time of war it assured her strength. More, the empire was France's sole tangible asset guaranteeing that in the postwar world her voice would continue to be heard at the highest international councils. Given time, she might rebuild her economy and forge the links of European community with the enormous power concentration this implied. But amid the wreckage of 1945, these possibilities seemed to lie in the remote future. The empire was to be the bridge from the present state of physical destruction to the nation's eventual rebirth in importance. In the new age of superpowers dominated by the United States and the Soviet Union, France could retain a semblance of rank and avoid incorporation as an American satellite only if she could speak with a voice that carried authority beyond the hexagon. Thus, at de Gaulle's bidding, the French delegates to the Hot Springs Conference early in 1945, and some months later to the San Francisco Conference, worked diligently to insure nonintervention guarantees sufficient to buffer the colonies from the interference of any international agency, such as that proposed by the United States. Indeed, at the London Council of Foreign Ministers in September, the French went so far as to support Italy's claims to Libya in order that their own neighboring possessions not be set a bad example. In the face of nationalist uprisings in Algeria, at Sétif, and in the Middle East, de Gaulle made clear his intention to maintain a world-wide French imperial presence.[5]

De Gaulle did not see his mastery of the art of realpolitik with its concern for national strength and greatness as an end in itself,

4. *Journal officiel,* May 15, 1945, p. 1049.
5. For this period, see Anton W. De Porte, *De Gaulle's Foreign Policy, 1944–1946* (Harvard University Press, Cambridge, 1968); and Marshall, *The French Colonial Myth,* Chapter 4.

however, but as a means in the service of the spiritual needs of France. As the General told President Franklin D. Roosevelt:

I know that you are preparing to aid France materially, and that aid will be invaluable to her. But it is in the political realm that she must recover her vigor, her self-reliance, and, consequently, her role. How can she do this if she is excluded from the organization of the great world powers and their decisions, if she loses her African and Asian territories—in short, if the settlement of the war definitively imposes upon her the psychology of the vanquished?[6]

This "psychology of the vanquished" had its origins in the deep-seated pessimism of the Third Republic and the conviction that in a profound sense France had been responsible for her own defeat by Germany. There had been the Rhineland, for example, then Munich, two occasions when French decadence—a combination of division, fear, treachery, and immobility—augured the coming of what Marc Bloch called the "strange defeat." Then came surrender and the Occupation when, as Jean-Paul Sartre put it, "all that London lived in pride, Paris lived in shame and despair."[7] Yet, at the same time, at the very depth of her humiliation, republican France began to stir, to fulfill Bloch's faith that "the deep-seated vitality of our people is intact and, sooner or later, will show signs of recovery."[8] These were the years of testaments of confidence in France, when André Malraux declared "I have married France"; when Albert Camus wrote his patriotic *Letters to a German Friend;* when Simone Weil expressed what an entire people felt:

Today every Frenchman knows what it is he missed as soon as France fell. He knows it as well as he knows what is missing when one is forced to go hungry. He knows that one part of his soul sticks so closely to France that when France is taken away it remains stuck to her, as the skin does to some burning object and is thus pulled off. There is something, then, to which a part of each Frenchman's soul sticks, and is the same for all, unique, real though impalpable, and real in the sense of something one is able to touch.[9]

6. Charles de Gaulle, *The Complete War Memoirs of Charles de Gaulle* (Simon and Schuster, New York, 1967), p. 574.
7. Jean-Paul Sartre, "La République du silence," reprinted in *Situations,* III (Gallimard, Paris, 1949). Sartre returned to this theme in his postwar novel *L'Age de raison.*
8. Marc Bloch, *Strange Defeat* (Norton, New York, 1968).
9. Simone Weil, *The Need for Roots* (Putnam and Sons, New York, 1952).

Of defeat and humiliation was born a nationalism of resurrection—a willingness to work and to sacrifice, combined with a confidence that France would emerge from the trial rejuvenated, welded at last into a unified national community, purged of the evil demons of self-doubt and despair of the prewar years, able to confront the future with new-found resolution.[10] It was the Resistance and the leadership of Charles de Gaulle which alone made possible these sentiments of pride and honor. The General was quite aware of the effect of his actions:

The collapse of 1940 and the capitulation that followed seemed to many monstrous and irremediable. The image of themselves the French had always had, the world's opinion of them, the testimony of history itself, had suddenly been abolished, annihilated. There was no opportunity for France to recover her dignity in her own eyes and in others' unless she took up arms again. But nothing was to help her recreate her unity and recover her prestige as much as this astonishing fact: that she could find in her scarcely mustered empire, in her persecuted nation, enough conviction and military valor to reconstitute an army.[11]

"France cannot be France without greatness," wrote de Gaulle in the most celebrated phrase of his *War Memoirs.* France, in other words, could only recover her self-confidence through standing up to the challenges which the world was sure to throw at her. In the process of affirming her greatness, she would recover a vigorous national identity, an indispensable element of collective action in the twentieth century. This is the spirit that Stanley Hoffmann has called the General's "Jacobinism exorcizing decadence"; he goes on to say that de Gaulle's "will to exorcize the demons of doubt and dispersion, of disorder and decline, that made him repeat that a great international undertaking was indispensable as much in response to 'what all the universe expects of us' as to 'what the self-esteem and hope of our people demands.' "[12]

10. The closest observers of the period describe the mood of these times in similar terms. See André Siegfried, *De la IIIè à la IVè République;* Raymond Aron, *Immuable et changeante;* and Stanley Hoffmann, "Paradoxes of the French Political Community," in Hoffmann et al., *In Search of France* (Harper and Row, New York, 1965).
11. De Gaulle, *The Complete War Memoirs,* p. 581.
12. Stanley Hoffmann, "Les Mémoires d'espoir," *Esprit,* December 1970, reprinted in Hoffmann, *Decline or Renewal? France since the 1930's* (Viking, New York, 1974).

But with the fatality of a Greek drama, this stirring crusade for national regeneration showed its tragic flaw in its excess of virtue. De Gaulle's fateful words sum up the disaster: "In Europe, in Africa, in Asia where France has suffered an unprecedented abasement, an astonishing recovery and an extraordinary combination of circumstances already offered her the opportunity to play a role in accord with her genius."[13]

For the General's error—equal in dimension only to the virtue of his intention—was to leave as his legacy to the Fourth Republic the major outlines of the policy which led to the war in Indochina. Henceforth, try as they would to free themselves from the humiliation of the disaster of 1940 through an ambitious imperial policy, the country's leaders would only bring more defeats upon the land. For the policy was an historical anachronism as soon as it was announced. And worse, the very conviction that they were responsible for their setbacks would incite the French to blame themselves for their reversals in the empire and so persist in their hopeless undertakings.

To be sure, the expected Gaullist retort to such a charge would be that it was neither the world, such as it was, nor the ambition, but the leadership of the Fourth Republic that brought the nation to disaster on the colonial question. As de Gaulle put it himself in a press conference on the problems of the war in Indochina in March 1949:

It is not only the forces and the matériel—however important they may well be—but there is also the mood, the confidence that one inspires, the clarity, the firmness of orders that one gives—or not—to those who confront local difficulties, in short the atmosphere in which one puts those who have a difficult task to fulfill, even sometimes to die, for France. The regime under which we live leaves very much to be desired in all this. It is a form of continual sabotage. . . . France needs a virile regime.[14]

Thus, not only did the General author the basic assumptions of a disastrous colonial policy; he dictated as well the terms by which the French would blame their system of government, and not

13. De Gaulle, *The Complete War Memoirs,* p. 931.
14. Charles de Gaulle, *Discours et messages: dans l'attente, 1946–1958* (Plon, Paris, 1970), pp. 278–279.

their ambitions, for their failure and so assure this policy a kind of self-perpetuating momentum.

Given the force of colonial nationalism, however, the policy which forecast a French return to Southeast Asia under the conditions of the General's Declaration of March 24, 1945, Relative to Indochina (see Chapter 3) was fundamentally unsound. Furthermore, de Gaulle's subsequent statements hardly confirm that it was the means at fault and not the ends. Thus, after two years of war in Indochina, the General warned that France must settle for nothing short of the terms of his March 1945 Declaration.[15] On March 29, 1949, he called for increased emphasis on a military solution, branded negotiation with Ho Chi Minh "capitulation," and announced his support of the puppet emperor Bao Dai.[16]

In regard to Algeria, de Gaulle's policy was equally reactionary. In April 1947, the General announced that Algeria should neither be assimilated into the Republic (on the model of the Antilles or Réunion), nor given its independence, but should be organized in such a manner that it could manage its own internal affairs. In August of the same year, during the debate over the Statute of Algeria (see Chapter 4), the General issued a Declaration in which, notably, he reneged on his own proposal of December 1943 (enacted by the Ordinance of March 7, 1944), which foresaw the gradual incorporation of Muslims into the first electoral college in favor of maintaining two clearly separate electoral colleges—one for the European minority, the other for the Muslims—in a French version of "separate but equal." He also spelled out those powers Paris must be careful to reserve to itself when granting Algeria a measure of autonomy.

French sovereignty: that means first that we cannot let it be put in question in any form, neither from within nor from without, that Algeria is in fact our domain. This means, moreover, that in no matter concerning Algeria can French public authorities—executive, legislative, judicial —alienate their right and their duty to be the last resort. This means, finally, that the authority of the French Republic must be exercised frankly and firmly there and that the governor general, who is invested by the state, will be responsible only before French public authorities.[17]

15. De Gaulle, *Dans l'attente,* p. 236.
16. De Gaulle, *Dans l'attente,* pp. 278–279.
17. De Gaulle, *Dans l'attente,* p. 107.

Having contributed handily to saddling France with an anachronistic, and therefore dangerous, program for Algeria, and having helped to weaken the government constituted to implement it, de Gaulle, speaking in Algiers, issued in October 1947 a grave warning against failure:

Any policy which . . . would have the effect of reducing the rights and duties of France here, or of discouraging the inhabitants of metropolitan origin who were and who remain the ferment of Algeria, or, finally, of letting the French Muslims believe that it could be allowable for them to separate their fate from that of France, would in truth only open the doors to decadence. . . . Loyal Frenchmen . . . know that in letting our cause be threatened upon this shore of the Mediterranean, it is the entire national edifice which risks dislocation.[18]

De Gaulle's "will to remake France one of the great world powers and to assure her a proud independence in regard to the other Greats," writes an admirer of the General, constituted "the essence of the Gaullist heritage. . . . Neither before nor after the departure of the General was there a real debate on the conditions of such an independence."[19] Any analysis which credits de Gaulle with saving republican government in France in 1958 from a fascistic military menace must surely balance its praise against his responsibility, and that of his supporters, for the perilous course on which he first fixed the Fourth Republic. His later reappraisal of French colonial policies, his intelligence and charismatic authority, and his commitment to republican government were precious assets to the French in the last years of the Algerian revolution. But our concern here is with the policy which first fixed France so self-destructively to her empire. On this count, too, his words and presence weighed heavily.

De Gaulle's policy had clear precedent in French history. Thus, the initial attack on Algiers in 1830 grew from a variety of sources, but one of the more decisive was the will to reassert national vigor after a period of international ostracism following the Napoleonic wars. Again, after the defeat by Bismarck in 1870, Jules Ferry, chief architect of the new French empire, urged his country to spiritual renewal through a policy of colonial expansion. A

18. De Gaulle, *Dans l'attente,* pp. 133–134.
19. Grosser, *La IVè République,* p. 33. Grosser is perhaps the leading authority on Fourth Republic foreign policy.

substitution of names and places makes passages from his famous parliamentary speech of 1885 strikingly similar to statements made after the defeat of World War II.

Must the containment forced on nations which experience great misfortunes result in abdication? Should we let ourselves be so absorbed by contemplating this incurable wound that we play no part in what is going on around us? Are we going to remain just as spectators and allow other peoples than ourselves to establish themselves in Tunisia, allow other peoples than ourselves to police the mouth of the Red River and . . . to dispute the mastery of the regions of Equatorial Africa. . . . It would mean that we would cease to be a first-rate power and become a third or fourth-rate power instead. Neither I, nor I imagine anyone here, can envisage such a destiny for our country. . . . If the French flag were taken from Tonkin, as some suggest for example, Germany or Spain would take our place in no time. . . . Is this the moment for France to go home, to fold in upon herself, to confine herself to a stationary policy, the politics of the fireside which in the next century will mark those people struck with inferiority or threatened by decadence? We dream for her of another destiny.[20]

In the same spirit, the great Socialist leader Jean Jaurès, an admirer of Ferry, could say in regard to the expansion of Algeria and the acquisition of Tunisia, "the empire made us lose two provinces, the Republic has given us two colonies."[21] The principal land of French settlement abroad, Algeria became the most important of the overseas possessions in terms of compensating for the loss of Alsace and Lorraine to the Germans. So Henri de Peyerimhoff, the respected official historian of Algerian colonization, stated the sentiment of many in 1906: "Mourning for the lost provinces gave birth to the dream of reconstituting others, greater and French. Public opinion, until now essentially preoccupied by the economics of the land, became more aware of the future of our race which here [in Algeria] was entrusted with our destiny."[22]

To be sure, colonial expansion had its critics, but the demon-

20. Cited in Henri Brunschwig, *French Colonialism, 1871–1914: Myths and Realities* (Praeger, New York, 1966), pp. 79–80.

21. Cited in Charles Robert Ageron, "Jaurès et les socialistes français devant la question algérienne (de 1895 à 1914)," *Le Mouvement Social*, XLII (January–March 1963), p. 5.

22. Henri de Peyerimhoff, *Enquête sur les résultats de la colonisation officielle de 1871 à 1895* (Torrent, Algiers, 1906), p. 41.

strated value of the empire during World War I settled the controversy for most. The most direct and immediate service of the empire had been in the provision of men and material. More than half a million men came from the colonies to fight for France, while even more arrived to take on jobs as industrial workers for the duration of the war. Over 200,000 of these men died for France.[23] The trade figures for the period following the outbreak of war reveal substantial contributions made by the empire in material terms as well. Previously, statistics show periods where first France, then the colonies, would have a trade surplus one with the other. But during and immediately after the war, the empire exported on the average perhaps twice as much to the metropole as it imported.[24]

Following World War I, French economic interests in the empire expanded. Between 1909 and 1913, the colonies absorbed 10 percent of France's exports and accounted for 12.9 percent of her imports. By 1931, these figures were 33 percent and 23 percent respectively.[25] Moreover, under the impetus of men like Albert Sarraut (author in 1923 of the influential *La Mise en valeur des colonies françaises*) and with the example of the spectacular development of Morocco during the interwar years, the awareness of the growing economic role of the empire in French affairs became far more widespread. Whatever the argument of learned economists, to the public mind the material importance of the empire to the nation appeared self-evident.

23. Estimates vary, but not greatly. See Pierre Varet, *Du Concours apporté à la France par ses colonies et pays de protectorat au cours de la Guerre de 1914* (Les Presses Modernes: Thèse pour le doctorat en science économique, Paris, 1927). For the debate over the value of the empire, see Raoul Girardet, *L'Idée coloniale en France* (La Table Ronde, Paris, 1972); and Jean Ganiage, *L'Expansion coloniale de la France sous la Troisième République* (Payot, Paris, 1968).

24. *Annuaire statistique de l'Union française,* 1892, published by the Ministère des Finances and the Ministère de la France d'Outre-Mer, shows a trade surplus with the colonies for every year of the preceding decade except for a very slight deficit in 1885. *Annuaire statistique,* 1921, shows a sharp rise in colonial exports to France relative to imports for the years 1915–1920. Algeria and North Africa always appear separately, however, and show different trends, except that during World War I this area also exported far more to France than it received (with the exception of 1916).

25. Raoul Girardet, "L'Apothéose de la 'plus grande France': l'idée coloniale devant l'opinion française (1930–1935)," *Revue Française de Science Politique,* XVIII (December 1968), p. 1089.

This was all the more true not for material, so much as for sentimental or symbolic, reasons. Whatever contribution the empire actually made to French prosperity and prestige after World War I (and while not negligible this was not decisive either), it was more in terms of what Overseas France, or Greater France, might render to the nation symbolically in the present and potentially in the future that its true importance lay.

Domestically, colonial expansion affected France in this regard by raising national consciousness and unity and thereby dampening the fires of class and cultural conflict. The competition with other powers for the possession of territory, the celebration of bold explorers and military officers, the evocation of French greatness in classroom texts, parades, and fairs became part of the collective conscience of the nation, a stimulus to national pride and solidarity.[26] For the bourgeoisie, the colonies offered the prospect of bureaucratic advancement and lucrative economic ventures. For the aristocratic and religious right, the empire was open territory for the development of the Church and for glorious military careers, reason enough to effect a reconciliation with the Republic.[27] Through these various images of what the empire could mean, a form of working colonial consensus was achieved during the interwar years which, in securing a commitment to possessions overseas, worked as well to gain a commitment to France.

But it was especially in terms of France's rank among the world powers that the colonies figured significantly. Raoul Girardet writes that in the interwar period the empire occupied a prominent place in regard "to certain major preoccupations, in the first order of which must certainly be put a tenacious uneasiness, at the time so strongly felt and so often expressed, that France could no longer keep her traditional rank as a great power in the contemporary world."[28] French Malthusian pessimism had set in with the

26. Manuela Semidei, "L'Empire français à travers les manuels scolaires," *Revue Française de Science Politique,* XVI (February 1966); Girardet, *L'Idée coloniale en France, passim.*
27. Nothing illustrates this better than the toast of Cardinal Lavigerie, spiritual authority of North Africa, to the French Navy visiting Algiers in 1890. Reprinted in David Thomson, ed., *France: Empire and Republic, 1850–1940: Historical Documents* (Macmillan, London, 1968), pp. 245–246.
28. Girardet, "L'Apothéose de la 'plus grande France,' " p. 1094.

defeat of 1870, and was exacerbated by World War I which took the lives of a generation of young Frenchmen. Through the Napoleonic wars, France had been the most populous and the richest state in Europe. Since then her leadership had been reduced, as Britain, then Germany, had outstripped her economically, while Britain, Germany, Russia, and, by the 1930's, Italy had become more populous.[29] From 1900 to 1939, the French population grew by only 3 percent, while that of Germany increased by 36 percent, that of Great Britain by 23 percent, that of Italy by 33 percent, and that of the United States by 72 percent. Even the meager French rate of 3 percent was deceiving, for virtually all of this came from immigration, while the figures in themselves did not express the manner in which an increasing part of the population was composed of the elderly.[30] One understands, then, something of the appeal of imperial slogans like "the France of one hundred million inhabitants" in a world where events seemed to conspire to reduce France to the level of Belgium, Switzerland, or Spain after the loss of her colonies. Just as the settlers in Algeria studded their references to the Muslim population with images of being "drowned" in human tides, so metropolitan France experienced the growth around her of nations "better confronting their destinies." The serious shortcomings of the stalemate political regime of the Third Republic only heightened the sentiment that the era of French greatness was fast drawing to a close.

In a fashion familiar in other countries as well, nationalism and imperialism thus fed each other in France.[31] Here is surely a part of the origin of de Gaulle's political inspiration during World War II. His emphasis on the unity of France being above factional disputes, and his pre-eminent concern that this unity be both achieved and expressed through an ambitious foreign policy, marked the highest point in the development of this concept in France. It would lead him naturally to an ambitious colonial policy after 1945.

29. Heinz Gollwitzer, *Europe in the Age of Imperialism, 1880–1914* (Harcourt, Brace and World, London, 1969), Chart p. 19.
30. Bernard Granotier, *Les Travailleurs immigrés en France* (Maspero, Paris, 1970), pp. 44–45.
31. Gollwitzer, *Europe in the Age of Imperialism,* Chapters 4 and 10.

Of course, one can overstate the extent to which the political consciousness of the Third Republic integrated colonial considerations into daily political discourse. On the one hand, the empire was relatively quiet and stable so that much more crucial domestic and European matters overshadowed colonial issues.[32] On the other hand, whatever sense of unity and security was obtained from a sense of empire was challenged during the interwar period by a new breed of colonial critics. Young native nationalists with connections in Paris, itinerant chroniclers like André Gide, and especially the new French Communist party created in 1920 at the Congress of Tours (and dedicated to determined anticolonialism by the 8th of the 21 Points for adhesion to the Third International), disturbed the French good conscience about the empire and even seemed to threaten its dislocation.

As the reaction of the French Socialist party suggests, however, such attacks seemed only to intensify the commitment to empire by making ardent reformers out of the non-Communist left.[33] As early as the 1907 Stuttgart Congress, the Second International had debated a motion in favor of supporting "positive" Western colonialism, defeating it by a narrow margin only after the strenuous objections of Karl Kautsky. A similar motion nevertheless gained the approval of the French party at Toulouse the following year. Despite the adamant dissent of a minority of the party (many of whom later went on to join the Third International), the majority felt that just as they were working for change in France through the established parliamentary system (Jaurès, *Evolution révolutionnaire*), so there was no contradiction in working for colonial reforms in the same manner. The eventual result of their effort would certainly be independence for the colonies, but in the interim the French left could protect the native populations both from international marauders and from oppressive local elites who would not hesitate to affirm their

32. During the interwar period, the chief disruptions were the discontent in Damascus, 1925–1926, the campaign against Abd el-Krim in the Rif Mountains, 1925–1927, and the troop mutiny and peasant uprisings in Tonkin, 1930–1931.

33. On Socialist colonial policy before World War II, see especially R. Thomas, "La Politique socialiste et le problème colonial de 1905 à 1920," *Revue Française d'Histoire d'Outre-Mer*, second trimester, 1960; Manuela Semedei, "Les Socialistes français et le problème colonial entre les deux guerres," *Revue Française de Science Politique*, XVIII (December 1968); Ageron, "Jaurès et les socialistes français."

presence should the French depart. On the balance, it could be maintained, French rule was less oppressive than that which preceded it, and in addition it had the potential to be influenced by Socialist ideas.[34] In this spirit, the mainstream of the party pushed not for independence but for the end of such colonial abuses as forced labor and called for the assimilation of native populations to democratic values and practices through the extension of modern education and civil liberties and by the creation of Socialist parties overseas.[35] Léon Blum summed up this position in an address before the Chamber of Deputies on June 10, 1927:

We do not accept that there is a right to conquest. . . . We will have accomplished what you call our civilizing mission the day that we will be able to restore the liberty and the sovereignty of the peoples whose territory we occupy. (Applause from the extreme left.) On the other hand, faced with a situation for which we are not responsible, to which we were always opposed, against which we have always obstinately fought, against which we will fight on every occasion, we will not content ourselves with a solution at once too simple and too dangerous consisting either in preaching insurrection and calling for a race war or in demanding immediate evacuation with all the dangers this holds for settlers and the natives themselves. (Very good, very good, from the left and extreme left.)[36]

In fact, Blum's rendition of history was somewhat inexact. The reconciliation of his party's internationalism with its national obligations had been effected some time earlier by Jaurès and had

34. Engels might even be cited on this point. As he wrote in 1848, on the occasion of the defeat of the Algerian leader Abd al-Qadir: "Upon the whole it is, in our opinion, very fortunate that the Arabian chief has been taken. . . . All these nations of free barbarians look very proud, noble, and glorious at a distance, but only come near them and you will find that they, as well as the more civilized nations, are ruled by the lust of gain and only employ ruder and more cruel means. After all, the modern bourgeois, with civilization, industry, order and at least relative enlightenment following him, is preferable to the feudal lord or to the marauding robber with the barbarian state of society to which they belong." Cited in Lewis Feuer, ed., *Marx and Engels, Basic Writings* (Anchor, New York, 1959), pp. 450–451. Mention might also be made of Thomas Ismail Urbain, an amazing Saint Simonist who worked tirelessly to bring to North Africa his version of humanistic socialism.

35. The Socialist use of the term assimilation connoted grafting modern (French) values and practices to the native system, not simply making Frenchmen of them.

36. *Journal officiel,* Chambre des Députés, June 10, 1927, p. 444.

been demonstrated not only by Socialist participation in World War I, but in the tacit acceptance by the majority of the party of the dream of imperial expansion.[37] In 1903, for example, Jaurès had declared: "I am convinced that France has interests of the first order in Morocco; I am convinced that these interests give her a form of right. . . . Yes, it is desirable in the interests of the natives of Morocco, as in the interests of France, that the economic and moral action of our country establishes and implants itself there."[38]

And again: "Our businessmen, our engineers have the right to pursue the peaceful action of France in China. We do not want to close off the outlets nor limit the influence of our country. French goods and French ideas must penetrate the great Chinese valleys just as the goods and ideas of other countries."[39]

More recently, Blum himself had supported the French expedition against Abd el-Krim in the Rif Mountains. Dissent within the SFIO had either been siphoned off to the Communist party in 1920, or, as in the case of Jean Zyromski, and later Charles Pivert and Daniel Guérin, the dissenters had simply been unable to shake the reformist convictions of the dominant majority.[40]

The election in 1936 of the Popular Front government with Blum at its head inaugurated a period of economic and administrative reform in the empire. Politically, however, the regime was more conservative. The looming menace of Adolf Hitler, the intransigent opposition of different settler organizations (particularly in Algeria), the press of serious domestic issues, and the toning down of Communist opposition on colonial matters all conspired to subvert programs of political reform (of which the

---

37. Jaurès' discussion of patriotism and his reconciliation of his nationalist and internationalist duties is strikingly reminiscent of Durkheim, who was writing at about the same time. Jaurès writes, for example, "The Patrie holds by its roots to the very center of human life and, if I may say so, to the physiology of men. . . . [There is] a collective conscience which has been formed and in which individual consciences are united and exalted," in *L'Armée nouvelle* (L'Humanité, Paris, 1915), pp. 448–449. And see as well Max Bonnafous, ed., *Oeuvres de Jean Jaurès* (Reider, Paris, 1933), I, 453–458.

38. Thomas, "La Politique socialiste," p. 240.

39. Bonnafous, ed., *Oeuvres*, p. 331.

40. See, for example, Daniel Guérin, *Au Service des colonisés, 1930–1953* (Editions de Minuit, Paris, 1954).

most important was the Léon Blum-Maurice Viollette proposal for Algeria). Instead, the Socialists would concentrate on economic and social affairs in the empire, thereby preparing the native peoples for the rights and obligations of political independence which were only momentarily to be postponed. As Marius Moutet, Socialist minister of the colonies, put it: "For us, colonization is the development of the masses who inhabit the colonies by raising their material, social, economic, intellectual, and cultural level. This is the first task of colonization. I consider it a mission, and in defending it, I believe that I am truly a minister of Revolutionary France."[41]

Thus, the Third Republic left in its legacy to the Fourth an agreement by the major political parties (with the exception of the Communists) that for France international greatness and domestic vitality were linked to one another and depended to an appreciable degree upon French influence in the preindustrial world. General de Gaulle's decision during World War II to peg his country's future domestic stability to its international rank, and to base this in turn in large measure on a revitalized empire had, therefore, its historical antecedents. As the General himself later recalled: "By the colonial epic [France] had sought to console herself for the loss of her far-away possessions in the eighteenth and nineteenth centuries, and then for her defeats in Europe in 1815 and 1870."[42]

In certain of its basic characteristics, then, the postwar colonial consensus actually depended on earlier thinking, when the SFIO had come to champion imperial reform as opposed to independence while the center-right had come to see imperial responsibilities as an aspect of national identity.[43] But it was de Gaulle's handling of these predilections which determined the importance of these modes of thinking after 1945. The failure of the Fourth Republic was its inability to break out of the terms of the colonial consensus once it was shown wanting.

41. *Journal officiel*, Chambre de Députés, December 15, 1936, pp. 3626–3627. Moutet's long colonial career stretched from before World War I until well after World War II. For his earlier position on Algeria, see Vincent Confer, *France and Algeria: The Problem of Civil and Political Reform, 1870–1920* (Syracuse University Press, Syracuse, 1966), pp. 100–110, 116–118.
42. Charles de Gaulle, *Mémoires d'espoir* (Plon, Paris, 1960), pp. 41–42.
43. See Marshall, *The French Colonial Myth*, Chapters 1 and 2.

3 Indochina and the Terms of the Colonial Consensus

The French certainly did not undertake the rejuvenation of their empire after 1945 with blind optimism that they would succeed. Their recent and serious defeat at the hands of Germany, the occupation by foreign powers of their overseas territories in the Levant, the Far East, and North Africa, the new rhetoric of anticolonial imperialism heard now from the United States as well as from the Soviet Union, and the markedly increasing political sophistication of local native elites were clearly recognized warnings that the future character of the empire was in doubt. The French thought, then, to parry these dangers through a series of firmly instituted reforms calculated to cement their rule by mobilizing popular support in the colonies for a continued French presence.

It is important to stress that this decision to reform in order to preserve (to use Edmund Burke's phrase) was in accord with the spirit of the Resistance. For once, apparently, realism in imperial affairs called for liberalism. The confidence that these reforms would preserve for France the power and prestige of the empire (soon to be renamed the French Union) seems to have depended on a set of interlocking assumptions. Foremost of these was the belief, widely shared in French political circles, that in their majority the colonial peoples appreciated the benefits of French rule, as they had demonstrated by their loyalty throughout the war. De Gaulle put it forcefully in a Washington press conference on July 10, 1944:

I ask each of you if he has not been struck by the fact that after four years of misfortunes and the occupation of France by the enemy, after four years of treason inside the country, not a single territory which was attached to France, not a single one, has refused the war effort for the liberation of France and the freedom of the world. I ask you to reflect on this since, speaking politically and humanly, it is, in my opinion, something very important for the future.[1]

In the same vein, no adjective appears so typically in the writing of the times as the word "loyal" (*fidèle*) to describe the character of the colonies.[2] As a reward for loyalty, the French would provide their overseas territories with funds for economic development and, more importantly, assure them new political rights and responsibilities commensurate with their maturity.

A second assumption was less precisely formulated than the first. It held that native elites would themselves come to see that their future interests lay in association with France. By pointing out the double menace any local ruling class would face alone— on the one hand from their own peoples whose political activity was tending to increase, on the other from rival industrial powers eager to take France's place—the French could persuasively maintain the existence of a harmony of interests binding their former empire to them. Interest as well as sentiment would create the bonds of postwar solidarity. Thus, Paris made an initial decision to support traditional over popular leaders, especially in Southeast Asia, in the lands of Laos, Cambodia, and Vietnam.[3]

But the French assumed as well that they would need to give immediate concrete evidence of the worth of the imperial connection. Following statements by de Gaulle in December 1943 of liberal intent toward Algeria and Indochina, a conference of high colonial officials convened at his instigation at Brazzaville, capital of what was then the French Congo, in order to draw up recommendations for the future Constituent National Assembly in

1. De Gaulle, *Pendant la guerre*, p. 419.
2. The pervasiveness of French confidence in colonial loyalty has been well-documented by William Wainwright, "De Gaulle and Indochina, 1940–1945" (unpublished doctoral thesis, the Fletcher School of Law and Diplomacy, Tufts University, 1971), Chapter 11.
3. A similar policy of working with local elites was suggested by Félix Eboué, governor general of French Equatorial Africa, himself from Guiana, in a program he began to circulate in 1941, eventually published under the title *La Nouvelle politique indigène pour l'Afrique Equatoriale Française.*

regard to colonial matters. Its most precise suggestions concerned economic issues where it stressed the development of the overseas areas through investment funds and education as well as the abolition of such practices as forced labor. Administratively, the Brazzaville Conference advocated the abolition of special native legal codes (the *indigénat*) and the increasing association of natives with the management of their respective countries. Politically, the Conference called for the extension of French civil liberties to the empire, metropolitan collaboration on a greater scale with traditionally recognized elites, native representation at the future French Constituent National Assembly, and the creation of a "French Federation" or "federal organization" which would promote in a systematic fashion the association of the various lands dependent on Paris. Far-reaching as these proposals seemed, the Conference reined them in with a preface that set forth the clear limits within which such reforms would occur: "The ends of the colonizing work accomplished by France in the colonies rule out any idea of autonomy, any possibility of evolution outside the French bloc of the empire; the eventual establishment, even in the future, of self-government in the colonies is out of question."[4]

To colonial Commissioner (and later Prime Minister) René Pleven, whose remarks followed de Gaulle's in opening the Conference, such a stipulation appeared self-evident: "In greater colonial France there are neither peoples to free nor racial discriminations to abolish. There are populations who feel French and who want to take, and to whom France wishes to give, a larger and larger part in the life and democratic institutions of the French community . . . but who do not expect to know any other independence than the independence of France."[5]

---

4. *Brazzaville: 30 janvier–8 février 1944*, published by the Ministère des Colonies, p. 32. As a practical obstacle to colonial emancipation, the report limited native promotion in the administrative structure: "the positions of command and direction shall admit only French citizens."

5. *Brazzaville*, p. 22. In his opening speech, de Gaulle stressed the military importance of the empire and the loyalty of the colonials to France, and then went on to state that, politically, France wanted these peoples to "s'élèver peu à peu jusqu'au niveau òu ils seront capable de participer chez eux à la gestion de leurs propres affairs." As usual, his word choice is instructive. Colonies will come "gradually" to "participate" in the "management" of "their own affairs" "at

Subsequent legislation fulfilled in substance the promises of Brazzaville. The provisional government purged the Vichy colonial bureaucracy, assigning more liberal administrators to top posts (for example, Yves Chatigneau, Eric Labonne, and Latrille). Decrees ir. 1945 arranged for colonial representation at the future Constituent National Assembly (64 seats out of 586 with about half going to settler deputies), while a series of laws and decrees from late 1945 until the fall of 1946 assured all colonial peoples the rights of French citizenship locally, at the same time abolishing forced labor and native legal codes. In April 1946 the Investment Fund for Economic and Social Development (FIDES) was voted in Paris, assuring the colonies much more serious support for their long-term economic development than had been the case under the Third Republic. Other official decisions dealt with the overseas territories individually. In March 1946 the "old colonies" of Guiana, Guadeloupe, Martinique, and Réunion became full French departments, while the Ordinance of March 7, 1944, relative to Algeria, and the Declaration of March 24, 1945, concerning Indochina, projected quite new political statutes to govern these areas. Finally, the Constituent National Assembly gave attention to the institutionalization of a parallel to the British Commonwealth which came to be known as the French Union.

Enlightened as these reforms doubtlessly appeared at the time in comparison with the colonial practices of Third Republic France, they were nonetheless substantially behind the demands being made by certain key nationalist leaders in the overseas territories. In the Levant, even before the end of World War II, independence movements cooperated with by the British had defeated de Gaulle's dogged efforts to maintain special French claims on Syria and Lebanon, under mandate to Paris since World War I.[6] In Madagascar, Morocco, and Tunisia, nationalists

---

home." That is, they will not "immediately" "govern" "independently," nor should they expect proportional representation in Paris or control over local issues of significance to France (military, diplomacy, economy). See de Gaulle, *Pendant la guerre,* pp. 370–373. Similarly, in July 1944, when a journalist asked him of Indochina, the General corrected the man by insisting that the appropriate word was "Indochinese Federation." *Pendant la guerre,* p. 419.

6. De Porte, *De Gaulle's Foreign Policy,* pp. 127–152.

had submitted programs to the French authorities calling for independence by 1946.[7] But it was in Indochina and Algeria that nationalists were advancing the most significant demands, for Algeria was by far the most important of France's overseas possessions, while Indochinese radicalism and determination threatened to set a pace for the entire empire. Liberal as the French reforms were, they could not match these calls for independence. Where the French authorities should be faulted, then, is not simply for their refusal to consider the possibility of the evolution of the colonies to independence, but also for their success in creating the illusion that enough had been done, that France had shown herself generous and needed now to show her resolve to remain sovereign.

Despite the contradictions between the French and nationalist positions, a brief moratorium, from the last months of the war throughout most of 1946, allowed the various parties involved time to clarify their positions. The nationalists were, to be sure, calling for independence, but even the Vietnamese were willing to negotiate the timing and character of such an agreement. For their part, the French were retreating behind the vague formula of "independence within the French Union," whose form the Constituent National Assembly to be elected in October 1945 would specify.

Seven months before this Assembly met, de Gaulle's provisional government issued the Declaration of March 24, 1945, whose terms provided for the political restructuring of French possessions in Southeast Asia after the surrender of Japan. At the time, of course, the Declaration could be interpreted as no more than a statement of intent, but in retrospect, this document appears to have been one of the most formative colonial position papers of the postwar period. According to its provisions, a governor general (named by Paris and assisted by appointed ministers responsible to him) and a Council of State would exercise effective legislative and executive control over an "Indochinese Federation" composed of the five countries of the region (Tonkin, Annam, Cochin China, Laos, and Cambodia). An Assembly

---

7. See Virginia Thompson and Richard Adloff, *The Malagasy Republic* (Stanford University Press, Stanford, 1965) and C. A. Julien, *L'Afrique du Nord en marche* (Julliard, Paris, 1952).

"elected according to the mode of suffrage the most appropriate to each of the countries" (a sop to traditional elites) would vote taxes, set the budget, and deliberate local laws and certain international accords. This Federation would, in turn, become integrated into the "federal organs" of the French Union with the rights and obligations such membership would entail. France would be in charge of Indochina's foreign relations, while the Union, in conjunction with Paris, could be expected to control the armed forces of the Indochinese Federation. Less clearly spelled out were the provisions for the internal organization of each of the five countries. The Declaration guaranteed civil liberties and assured each country that it would "keep its own character inside the Federation."[8]

Fast-paced events seemed for the moment, however, to make this program for the future of Indochina politically irrelevant. On March 9, 1945, the Japanese had ousted the Vichy administration in charge of the area, replacing it with their own direct control. The Potsdam Agreement of July, provided for the British to accept the Japanese surrender in Vietnam south of the 16th parallel, while the Kuomintang forces would occupy the country to the north. Meanwhile, the Vietminh cadres under Ho Chi Minh and General Vo Nguyen Giap had increased their military preparations and intensified the political mobilization of the country behind their banner. With the defeat of Japan in August, Ho entered Hanoi, while an army under his associate Tran Van Giau moved to take Saigon. On September 2, 1945, Ho proclaimed Vietnamese independence. The French Declaration of March 24 appeared dated less than six months after its issue.

Back in Paris, the victory of the left at the elections to the First Constituent National Assembly in October 1945 (302 of the 596 seats were won by Socialists or Communists) produced a majority favorable to a liberal interpretation of the future of the empire.[9]

8. The text of the Declaration is reprinted in Charles de Gaulle, *Mémoires de guerre: le salut, 1944–1946* (Plon, Paris, 1959), pp. 458–460.

9. For a thorough account of constitution-making in regard to the empire, see Marshall, *The French Colonial Myth*, Chapters 7–9. Also, Gordon Wright, *The Reshaping of French Democracy* (Reynall and Hitchcock, New York, 1948) *passim;* François Borella, *L'Evolution politique et juridique de l'Union française depuis 1946* (Librairie Générale de Droit et de Jurisprudence, Paris, 1958); and Pierre François Gonidec, *Droit d'outre-mer, I: de l'empire coloniale de la France à la communauté* (Montchrestien, Paris, 1959).

As elaborated in the Constitution this Assembly drafted, the French Union would be built from the bottom up. Local assemblies would first be created and they, in turn, would send delegates to Paris to determine the qualities of the Union and to define the specific character of the attachment of the various states and territories to the Federation and to France. In the interim, colonial deputies would continue to sit in the French National Assembly. It should be emphasized that this was no plan for decolonization, no proof that Socialists as well as Communists were preparing to cut the imperial connection and devolve power to these territorial assemblies. To the contrary, the left maintained, with some naiveté, that such a liberal creation of the Union would guarantee the stability and longevity of the postwar empire.[10]

The scheme was left untried, for the electorate refused this draft constitution in the referendum of May 5, 1946. Thanks to a bare majority of Communists and Socialists, joined by the Algerian nationalist Ferhat Abbas, the Constitutional Commission of the Second Constituent National Assembly elected in June agreed initially on a text for the establishment of the French Union similar in spirit to the provisions contained in the rejected draft. But other deputies on the Commission opposed this notion of the colonial peoples themselves determining the character of the Union. They proposed instead that a strong central framework be spelled out giving dominant authority to France. Within this structure local reforms could proceed so long as they did not jeopardize the stability of the Union itself. Eventually this minority position gained powerful support from outside the Commission, and ultimately it prevailed. Title VIII of the Constitution as adopted was the product of their labors.

It was negotiations with the Vietminh at Fontainebleau in July 1946 over the future status of Indochina which may be taken as the occasion first galvanizing official French opinion to insist that the terms of the eventual French Union not open the metropole to the loss of its overseas possessions. The decision was crucial, for

10. See especially the speeches made by Socialist and Communist deputies during the Second Constituent National Assembly, *Journal officiel*, September 18, 1946, by which time their positions had been subjected to a withering attack, especially by de Gaulle.

although de Gaulle had insisted the preceding August that France would preserve her sovereignty over Indochina (as had been clearly intended by his March 1945 Declaration), and although the French had launched a coup in Saigon on September 23, 1945, to remove the city from Vietminh control, the Agreement of March 6, 1946, between what was acknowledged as the government of Vietnam, signed for by Ho Chi Minh, and the French government represented by Jean Sainteny, had reintroduced an element of caution and realism into the French view of Indochina.[11] Previously, late in February 1946, the French had reached an understanding with the Chinese calling for the rapid evacuation of the North by the Kuomintang forces in return for the transfer of French rights and possessions in China to the government of Chiang Kai-shek.[12] The subsequent Agreement of March 6, between Ho and the French, provided for the return of a small French army to North Vietnam but limited its occupation to five years and recognized "the Republic of Vietnam as a free state having its government, its parliament, its army, and its finances and forming part of the Indochinese Federation and the French Union." It also determined that a referendum in Cochin China would decide the question of the reunification of this area to the two northern provinces (the Ky of Annam and Tonkin), since it had been administratively and historically distinct under French rule. The ambiguity of the accord lay in the wording of the formula "free state . . . part of the Indochinese Federation and the French Union" and in the concluding clause calling for immediate negotiations on "the diplomatic relations between Vietnam and foreign states, the future status of Indochina, and economic and cultural interests."[13] The Fontainebleau Confer-

11. On August 24, 1945, de Gaulle stated in Washington, "The French position in Indochina is very simple. France intends to recover her sovereignty over Indochina. Of course this re-establishment will be accompanied by a new regime, but for us sovereignty is the capital issue." *Pendant la guerre,* p. 605.

12. Allan B. Cole, ed., *Conflict in Indo-China and International Repercussions: A Documentary History, 1945–1955* (Cornell University Press, Ithaca, 1956), pp. 7ff.

13. The text of this Agreement appears in English in Marvin E. Gettleman, ed., *Vietnam* (Fawcett, New York, 1965), p. 61, omitting, however, an appended accord on the conditions for the return of French troops to the North. The text in French with this accord is reprinted in Philippe Devillers, *Histoire du Viet-Nam de 1940 à 1952* (Seuil, Paris, 1952), pp. 225–226.

ence of July and August 1946 was to clarify, then, the sense of the Agreement of March 6.

Even before Fontainebleau, the first Dalat Conference called by the high commissioner of Indochina, Thierry d'Argenlieu, and the terms of the agreements reached between the rulers of Laos and Cambodia with the returning French armies suggested that Paris was in no mood to equivocate on the re-establishment of her sovereignty in Southeast Asia. Fontainebleau confirmed this. In essence, the French position here represented a choice for the Declaration of March 24, 1945, over the recently concluded and more liberal provisions of the Agreement of March 6, 1946: Vietnam would be neither united nor independent. Cochin China would continue to be separate from the two northern provinces (Annam and Tonkin), while the French negotiators defined the political, military, and economic obligations of the Ho Chi Minh government within the Indochinese Federation and the nascent French Union in such a manner that French sovereignty over the area would in practice be virtually uncontestable. When commentators would later seek to absolve France from responsibility in initiating the conflict in Vietnam, claiming ignorance, indecisiveness, and lack of a policy to be at fault, one wonders if they had perhaps forgotten the record of this two-month conference held just outside the French capital during the summer of 1946.[14]

Other events were likewise conspiring to strengthen the position of those opposed to a liberal formulation of the French Union. From July 20 until August 24, 1946, a colonial congress, the "Etats Généraux de la Colonisation Française," was meeting in Paris, adding its deliberations to the pressures of the Fontainebleau Conference on the deputies of the Constitutional Commission who were engaged in drafting the articles relevant to the Union. Then, on August 27, came two important statements on the future of the empire, one by General de Gaulle, the other by the prominent Radical leader Edouard Herriot. Since June, de

---

14. For a good, brief account of the Conference, see Devillers, *Histoire du Viet-Nam*, Chapter 17; also Ellen Hammer, *The Struggle for Indochina, 1940–1955* (Stanford University Press, Stanford, 1967), Chapter 7. For a more complete account, see Henri Azeau, *Ho Chi Minh, dernière chance: la conférence franco-vietnamienne de Fontainebleau, juillet 1946* (Flammarion, Paris, 1968).

Gaulle had made it evident that he was concerned that the French overseas territories not be lost through the ineptitude of party politics. On August 27, the General issued a press statement in which he underscored the vital importance to France of the empire, spelled out the essential powers France must preserve in the future Union, and outlined the institutional prerequisites of a successful federation on these terms. "United to the overseas territories which she has opened to civilization, France is a great power," he declared. "Without these territories she risks being one no longer. Everything directs us to organize on a new but precise basis the relations between the metropole and the people of all races who are linked to her destiny."[15] The same day, Herriot delivered an influential address before the Constituent National Assembly in which he concluded on a note of concern that was to sound like a leitmotif throughout the life of the Fourth Republic:

The world today is completely divided up. There is no frozen land near the poles, there is no burning Pacific island where some nation has not planted its flag. Where will there remain a place for France? Am I wrong to tell you then that the problem I have just evoked is, for our country, for the overseas territories as for the metropole, a question of life and death?[16]

Appearing before the Constitutional Commission on September 11, the Socialist Minister of Colonies Marius Moutet recalled Herriot's speech and called upon the deputies to give more structure to their concept of the French Union, being especially precise on the role France was to play therein. He proposed for consideration a text quite different from the one the Commission was drafting. On September 12, his proposal was accepted, but not without opposition from the left which was stilled only when Prime Minister Georges Bidault made a dramatic appearance before the Commission, threatening to stake his government's life on the content of this text.[17] In rapid order, the Commission adopted the government's text, and the Assembly voted the arti-

15. De Gaulle, *Dans l'attente*, pp. 18–23.
16. *Journal officiel*, August 27, 1946, p. 3336.
17. *Journal officiel*, September 11, 1946 (Moutet); September 18, 1946 (Bidault).

cles of Title VIII of the Constitution relative to the French Union.[18]

Experts in jurisprudence have convincingly pointed out the ambiguity and contradictions with which the final text of the Constitution providing for the French Union abounds.[19] Its one central feature stands out clearly enough, however: the authority of France over the Union was beyond dispute. Neither immediately nor in the future would there be a partnership among equals within this federation. The only significant power whatsoever conferred on the Union was that of pooling members' resources for the common defense (Article 62). And here, "The government of the Republic shall undertake the coordination of these resources and the direction of the policy appropriate to prepare and ensure this defense." In legislative matters, the Union was totally subordinate to the National Assembly (Articles 71–72). Nor could foreign nationalists convert the Union into a platform from which to dislodge France from her overseas positions, for its key institutions (the presidency, the high council, and the assembly) were safely under metropolitan control (Articles 62–66). Separate legislative acts under the competence of the National Assembly, not the Union, were to determine the composition and competence of the local assemblies of the various territories and decide the position of the associated states within the Union (Articles 61 and 77). As at Brazzaville two and a half years earlier, there was to be no thought of self-government, even in the future.

The tedious debates over whether it was the "assimilationist" or the "federalist" aspects of the Union which predominated can be both absurd and misleading. They are absurd when they direct attention away from the chief features of the institution, its powerlessness and subordination to Paris, and they are misleading when they throw a smoke screen over the way these supposedly opposed aspects actually could work in unison. For, properly coordinated, the assimilationist and federalist clauses of the mea-

18. The text of the Constitution in English is reprinted in Philip Williams, *Crisis and Compromise,* Appendix 1.

19. Gonidec, *Droit d'outre-mer,* pp. 334ff; Borella, *L'Evolution politique, passim;* Grosser, *La IVè République,* pp. 247–251; and Marshall, *The French Colonial Myth,* Chapters 8 and 9.

sure canceled out in each other any progressive element that either alone might have possessed. By pleading federalism, the French could avoid paying the intolerable price of true assimilation—proportional representation in the National Assembly and heavy subsidies for economic development. By pleading assimilation, on the other hand, the French could assure that the federal union and the local assemblies could never gain the power to pull the empire apart centrifugally. It is often said that French thinking and practice were contradictory in regard to the colonies. What must be appreciated is how this supposed contradiction actually worked to keep the overseas possessions French. The true contradiction in French policy was elsewhere: Paris would be both liberal and sovereign abroad. When the chips were down, when a choice had to be made either to be liberal and grant independence or to be sovereign and repress colonial nationalism, France would choose the latter.

The moment of decision was not long in coming. Within three months of the adoption of the text creating the French Union, the government was using its terms to justify a policy of force in Indochina. The Fontainebleau Conference had closed with the signing of a *modus vivendi* between the French and the Vietnamese; agreement on the essential issues dividing the two sides was as distant as it had ever been. Low-level fighting between the French and Vietminh forces had continued in South Vietnam since the coup in Saigon in September 1945, and had commenced in North Vietnam as well, after the French landing there the following March. Moreover, High Commissioner d'Argenlieu's decision to convene a second Dalat Conference in August 1946, designed to spell out the terms of the Indochinese Federation, and his continued support for an autonomous government of Cochin China after the suicide of its first president, belied expectations that a satisfactory political settlement could soon be reached. On November 23, 1946, the conflict sharply worsened when the French bombarded the Vietnamese quarter of Haiphong following a series of provocations. The French subsequently demanded the retreat of Vietminh troops from the area of Haiphong, and on December 19, they ordered the disarmament of the Vietminh militia in Hanoi. That night came the Vietminh riposte. The war was on.

Commentators at all sympathetic to the French have seldom failed to dwell on the matter of a certain telegram sent by Ho to Blum that never arrived, or on the general ignorance and disinterest of the French government in Southeast Asian affairs, or on the high-handedness of military officials on the scene as accountable for Paris backing into this disastrous conflict. To cite a prime example, we are told that French leaders were unaware of the attack of their own forces on November 23, and so dated the commencement of hostilities as December 19, making the Vietminh the clear aggressors. Yet all these instances of ignorance, accident, and miscalculation cannot conceal the fact that by the winter of 1946 a clash between the French and the Vietnamese seemed well-nigh inevitable. Georgette Elgey, for instance, has certainly damaged the reputation of General Philippe Leclerc, one of the alleged heroes of realism who supposedly knew better than to get involved in a conflict in Southeast Asia, when she reports a confidential letter he wrote to Maurice Schumann about the time of the Fontainebleau Conference:

> In Indochina, France has won. We need a bit more time before order will be completely restored. . . . Who is Ho Chi Minh? We must not forget before anything else that he is a great enemy of France and that the goal pursued by him and his party six months ago was to throw us out pure and simple. . . . The framework fixed by France [at Fontainebleau] is perfectly clear and well defined: Indochinese Federation within the framework of the French Union. It is necessary that our representatives maintain this.[20]

As for the bombardment of Haiphong on November 23, Elgey is categoric: "One fact is certain: all those responsible, from Monsieur Moutet to Admiral Thierry d'Argenlieu and General Leclerc approved it."[21]

Once again, then, we are back to the colonial consensus, to the unity of ends which underlay the later division on means, to the determination that Indochina remain effectively French. Certainly there were important exceptions. This was not the position of the French Communist party, nor of such Socialists as Paul Rivet and Léon Boutbien, nor of a handful of observers like Paul

20. Georgette Elgey, *La République des illusions, 1945–1951* (Fayard, Paris, 1965), pp. 161–162.
21. Elgey, *La République*, p. 168.

Mus, Colonel Bernard, Raymond Aron, or the editors of *Les Temps Modernes*. But the acts of a Socialist government in power during the months succeeding the commencement of large-scale fighting provide the surest indication that more than inadvertence was involved in the genesis of the conflict.

This new phase of hostilities found the aging Socialist leader Léon Blum once again for a short while prime minister of France. In an important speech before the National Assembly on December 23, 1946, Blum declared:

> The old colonial system which established possession by conquest and maintained it by constraint, and which aimed at the exploitation of the peoples and the lands conquered, is today out of date. . . . According to our Republican doctrine, colonial possession reaches its final goal and finds its true justification only the day it ends, that is to say, the day when the colonial people have been made able to live fully free and to govern themselves. The reward of the colonizing people is then to have given rise to sentiments of gratitude and affection in the colonized people. . . . Once this crisis is surmounted, our goal shall remain exactly the same. . . . We must take up the work now interrupted, that is, the organization of a free Vietnam in an Indochinese Union freely associated with the French Union. But first of all, peaceful order, the necessary base for the execution of contracts, must be restored.[22]

Virtually all the essential aspects of French republican colonial doctrine were hereby announced in the first hour of trial. With this speech, Blum rallied to de Gaulle's formula for the future of Indochina under French sovereignty—membership in the Indochinese Federation and the French Union—justified it in terms of French humanistic pretensions, and supported it with a call to arms. Nearly a year later, when he was surely better informed and no longer laboring under the pressure of leading the country, Blum made a bid to return to power, attacking with equal vigor the nationalist fanatics and colonialist exploitation in Indochina. Together, he said, they were corrupting "an atmosphere of mutual confidence, solidarity, and affection" that he felt should exist "between France and the peoples who are to associate with her in the French Union."[23] Again the question arises: was the system to blame for French colonial reversals with all the problems with

22. *L'Année politique,* 1946, p. 545.
23. *L'Année politique,* 1947, p. 330.

which it is customarily associated, or was it rather a policy that gained the support of a decisive majority of the French political elite which was at fault?

In January 1947, another Socialist, Paul Ramadier, succeeded Blum as prime minister. In his investiture speech, Ramadier made it clear that France would not tolerate rebel aggression against what he called "the historic work of eternal France."[24] On March 18, during a debate over Indochina, Ramadier unilaterally denounced the Agreement of March 6, 1946 (although in essence this had already been effected by the Fontainebleau and Dalat Conferences), claiming that the Constitution of the Fourth Republic now officially abrogated this earlier accord. Henceforth, for Vietnam it was a question of "independence within the framework of the French Union. . . . Today it is no longer a matter of the framework of the treaty of March 6." And France would fight, he said: "We cannot accept peace and order being disturbed. We must protect the lives and possessions of the French, the foreigners, and our Indochinese friends who have shown their confidence in French liberty." Let it be known, he concluded, that "France must remain in Indochina, that her replacement there is not open, and that she must continue her civilizing work."[25]

Another Socialist, Minister of Overseas France Marius Moutet, had already prepared the public for Ramadier's announcement, stating on January 4, 1947, that "before any negotiation, it is now necessary to have a military victory. I regret it, but we cannot let anyone get away unpunished with such madness as the Vietminh have shown." And four months later: "We will certainly not negotiate with those who have no other purpose than to chase us out by all means and for whom new accords would only be an armistice and a way to continue the struggle. Nor even more will we negotiate with those who have carried out a policy of systematic terrorism."[26]

The ultimate sanction for French action came to lie with Title VIII of the Constitution, which provided for the French Union. Emile Bollaert, appointed high commissioner in Indochina by the

24. *L'Année politique,* 1947, p. 322.
25. *Journal officiel,* March 18, 1947, pp. 904–906.
26. *L'Année politique,* 1947, pp. 426–427.

Ramadier government in an effort to replace the reactionary d'Argenlieu with a man considered to be progressive, put this liberal concept appropriately well in a speech he delivered on May 15, 1947:

One must recognize that the notion of independence, even if one remains attached to it sentimentally, has changed in content. It is rather of interdependence that one must speak. I fear that those responsible for the present catastrophe in taking arms against the French Union [*sic*] have entered their country into a backwards evolution which goes against the ineluctable evolution of humanity toward progress. In the face of an enfeebling separatism, the concept of the French Union realizes the most perfect type of association there is. . . . The era of empires is over. The era of friendship must begin.

Four months later he repeated: "Liberty within the French Union: this liberty is the foundation of the future relations between France and the people of Indochina. It has no limits but those imposed by the membership of these territories in the French Union." Bollaert then specified that this meant leaving all military and diplomatic powers to Paris as well as certain economic and political matters. On the same day Bollaert spoke in Indochina, Ramadier and Moutet issued a statement in Paris underscoring the complete agreement of the government with the declaration.[27]

27. *L'Année politique,* 1947, pp. 275, 360.

4 Background to the Consensus on Algeria

Indochina was not the only colonial issue on which Ramadier's Socialist government was to leave its imprint. He named tough old General Juin to replace the liberal resident minister of Morocco, Eric Labonne. Thereafter, relations between France and the Moroccan nationalists steadily deteriorated. Ramadier also gave unstinting support to the fierce suppression of the Madagascan uprising of March–April 1947 (official reports estimated over 80,000 Madagascans killed) and to its sequel in the arrest and prosecution of the Madagascan deputies to the National Assembly. And Ramadier was prime minister when the National Assembly voted a bill in the summer of 1947 designed to restructure Algeria politically. This basic document was known as the Statute of Algeria of 1947.

The importance of drafting the Statute was that it obliged the French to face the potential contradiction between their desire to establish a liberal regime in Algeria corresponding to democratic principles, and their concern that Algeria remain French. The danger was obviously that a Muslim population, accorded the right to select its representatives, who in turn would wield genuine political power, might well decide to declare its independence from France. The prewar Popular Front government of Léon Blum and de Gaulle's wartime provisional government had both recognized the genuine need to formulate a political structure to deal with Muslim nationalism, but in each case the press of other political demands had resulted in postponement. However, according to an understanding reached during the Second Constituent Assembly, one of the first responsibilities of the first legislature of the Fourth Republic would be to define the exact political status of Algeria, provide for the division of powers between Algiers and Paris, and establish the local rights and responsibilities of the Muslim and settler populations of the three North African departments. The intention was therefore to legislate a form of Home Rule bill for Algeria that would permit the local population more control of its own affairs, recognize the distinctiveness of the Algerian personality by according new rights to the Muslim culture, and determine the character of the ties between France and Algeria anew.

Although four principal groups submitted drafts of a bill to serve as a basis for discussing the projected Statute of Algeria, essentially there were two positions. On the one side were the proposals of the Socialists and the government (which, despite its Socialist prime minister and interior minister, revived Bidault's drafts presented at the end of the Second Constituent Assembly). Each of these bills called for genuine administrative and political reforms in favor of the Muslim community, but at the same time unequivocally reaffirmed French sovereignty over Algeria. On the other side were the proposals of the French Communist party (PCF) and Ferhat Abbas' UDMA (Union Démocratique du Manifeste Algérien) which had in common the prospect of self-government for Algeria, although the PCF hedged this with more reservations of time and form than did the UDMA. The distinction between these two positions is fundamental, for while the proposals of the Socialist government remained bedeviled by the contradiction between being liberal and staying sovereign in Algeria, the Communist draft both recognized the problem and provided for a liberal solution should a choice have to be made.[1]

The Communist proposal called, most notably, for the election

1. For the complete texts of these various projects see *Notes et Etudes Documentaires*, a French government publication, number 684 (1947). The UDMA proposal, first submitted in August 1946, called for the immediate creation of an "Algerian Republic," opposed voting by a double electoral college, and admitted the right of France to determine Algerian diplomatic and defense policy only "in common with" Algeria.

by universal suffrage every four years of an Algerian Assembly which would in turn select a prime minister who would name the ministers of the Algerian government that he would form (Articles 23, 34–39). For a period of five years (or two elections) after the bill became law, Algeria would continue to be divided into two equal electoral colleges—one Muslim, one French—allowing thereby a transition period of eight years (in addition to the time it would take to put the Statute into effect) before the Muslim popular majority would make its full weight felt. The Assembly would "alone exercise legislative power over the totality of Algerian internal questions. This power cannot be delegated" (Article 23). The proposal recognized French control over Algerian diplomacy and defense, and made a place for a representative of Paris who would pass on Algerian foreign trade (Articles 43–44). Finally, Algeria would be a member of the French Union, initially as an associated territory, eventually as an associated state.

The text was, of course, open to amendment, but in its essential features it had obvious strengths, both practical and moral. Alone of the French parties, the Communists were willing to be genuinely democratic in Algeria and to accept the consequences of this position, even if it should ultimately lead to Algerian independence. As the Communists never tired of repeating, "the right to divorce does not imply the obligation to do so." However, the Communists of 1945–1947 were not the militant anti-colonialists of 1925–1927 (the period of the Rif War). But at least since the elections of June 2, 1946, to the Second Constituent Assembly, the PCF and its Algerian ally the PCA (Algerian Communist party) had recognized that there could be no mating of communism and nationalism in North Africa unless the right to independence was backed unequivocally.[2]

The Communists nevertheless had two major reasons to support the preservation of French influence in Algeria. First, as elsewhere in Africa where local communists benefited from its aid, the PCF wanted the French presence to help curb the growing power of non-Marxist nationalists. In the case of Algeria, this meant a policy of opposition to Messali Hadj, the Algerian Popu-

2. Emmanuel Sivan, *Communisme et nationalisme en Algérie, 1920–1962* (Presses de la Fondation Nationale des Sciences Politiques, Paris, 1976), pp. 154–161.

list leader in favor of the PCA. Secondly, the Communist party preferred that France, rather than the United States, be the preeminent foreign power in North Africa. In this same spirit, the Communists had rallied earlier to de Gaulle's defense of French prerogatives in the Levant, for they were as worried as any other political group in France that the Anglo-Americans would move into any position abandoned by France.[3] There was a third reason as well. The Communists sensed the determination of France to remain in Algeria and decided not to sacrifice here the leverage that might be needed on issues they deemed more important, such as postwar Western policy toward Germany. It is, of course, still possible to criticize the lack of vigor with which the PCF supported the cause of Algerian liberation—as indeed many Algerian nationalists and men like Sartre were later to do. But it is far from the facts to pretend, as a host of writers have, that because the Communist party initially supported the repression of the Sétif uprising in May 1945, or voted Mollet emergency powers for Algeria in 1956, it was procolonial, or at the least unwilling to adopt a clear anticolonial stand. To be sure, it favored decolonization under certain terms rather than others. And since the party was isolated in its anticolonialism, it at times played its position down in order to obtain allies on other matters the party deemed more urgent. But not to respect the distance of the PCF from the other major political formations in France is to obscure an important aspect of the colonial consensus by making it seem that the consensus was unselfconsciously accepted by all.[4]

By contrast, the Socialist proposal for the Statute of Algeria betrayed once again in microcosm the contradiction besetting

3. For example, Florimond Bonte could say before the Consultative Assembly: "Installed in Algiers and in Tunis as well as in Marseilles, France is guardian of the great interests of civilization and of a necessary equilibrium in the eastern Mediterranean. She cannot without danger underestimate the importance of her role in the Mediterranean. She is and must remain a great power in Africa. (Applause.) Greater France has 110 million inhabitants and unlimited resources. Thus we need never feel crushed by an inferiority complex (Very good, very good) which might push us into considering our country as an appendage, a complement to other states." *Journal officiel,* November 21, 1944, p. 311.

4. Non-Communist writers are only now beginning to make these distinctions. See Irwin M. Wall, "The French Communists and the Algerian War," *Journal of Contemporary History,* XII (July 1977).

republican France long before the shortcomings of the Fourth Republic's political system began to take their toll: the Socialists would be liberal in Algeria, but France would be sovereign there as well. As Moutet had put it in an exchange with Abbas before the Constitutional Commission, the goals appeared complementary: "The more Algeria is a French department, the more we march in the direction of Algerian emancipation."[5] A primary concern of the Socialists, then, was that French sovereignty not be jeopardized. Their draft Statute was faithful to this end by providing for an Algerian Assembly whose competence extended only to taxes and the budget and to tailoring laws passed in Paris to fit the Algerian situation. True authority in the land remained with the governor general, promoted to the rank of minister of Algeria, who was responsible only to Paris and who, with the prefects named with his approval by the French Cabinet, controlled in turn the various services in Algeria. Articles 15 and 16 of the proposed Statute gave both the minister and the National Assembly the power to determine whether the Algerian Assembly exceeded its competence.

Yet, the Socialists would be liberal as well. After a transition period of unspecified length, universal single electoral college voting would replace the dual college system in elections to the Algerian Assembly and, presumably, to the National Assembly as well (Articles 2 and 8). This promised considerably to augment the local power of the Muslim community. At the same time, the bill's preface made pious but vague references to the worth of Muslim civilization. While this allowed the Socialists to discount the seriousness of suggestions that Algeria be assimilated into the Republic, it also allowed them to restrict North African representation in Paris.[6]

The chief difference between the Socialist proposal and that of the government, which was eventually adopted, lay in the latter's preservation of the dual electoral college. Subsequent colonialist agitation managed to make this even more rigid by disqualifying from membership in the first European college certain categories of Muslims whom General de Gaulle had admitted with the

5. *Journal officiel,* September 11, 1946, p. 499.
6. *Notes et Etudes Documentaires,* number 684 (1947).

Ordinance of March 1944.[7] Certain commentators, both at the time and since, have criticized the Socialist ministers in power for abandoning the text of their party and giving in to certain colonialist demands for revision of the Statute.[8] But surely this misses the point. The Socialist fault lay not so much in capitulating on certain specific reforms as in the inability to see beyond reformism. What needed to be grasped was the possible antagonism between liberal and sovereign principles in Algeria. This, among the major metropolitan parties, only the PCF seemed to grasp. But Cold War mentality has apparently so pervaded academic writing that the Communists do not receive due credit. In the process, the true shortcoming in Socialist policy necessarily passes unmentioned.

As finally adopted, the Statute of Algeria created a two-college Assembly, thereby giving the European 10 percent of the population parity with the Muslim 90 percent. In addition, according to Article 39, a quarter of the deputies (or the governor general or the financial commission) could demand that any measure proposed be passed by a two-thirds majority, in effect giving a veto power to the settler deputies. But it was unlikely the veto would prove necessary. Aside from the right to raise revenues locally and deliberate the budget, the Assembly had little power. On fundamental economic, political, and juridical matters, power remained vested in Paris. Authority locally was concentrated in the hands of the governor general (who was responsible only to the Cabinet in Paris) and the government council (responsible only to the governor).

Weak as the Statute was, it was nevertheless sabotaged in a series of administrative and parliamentary maneuvers, and, as early as 1947, was unable to reconcile political liberality in Algeria with continued French sovereignty there. To examine why this was the case takes us from the political situation in France to that existing in North Africa in the aftermath of World War II.

In order to assess the wisdom of the 1947 Statute of Algeria, we must raise the question of whether there were political and eco-

7. De Gaulle himself approved this revision. See his Declaration of August 18, 1947, reprinted in *Dans l'attente.*
8. For example, Oppermann, *Le Problème algérien,* Chapter 4; Robert Aron, *Les Origines de la Guerre d'Algérie* (Fayard, Paris, 1962), pp. 259–289.

nomic reforms that France might have promoted in North Africa, not only in the decades before the revolution began but even after its outbreak, which might have influenced decisively the character of the uprising or even preserved French sovereignty there. Failing this, might the independence of Algeria have been secured in other circumstances, with less human suffering or under different nationalist leaders than was the case? Or is it enough to consult economic indicators or to allude to some mysterious spirit of the times ("the wave of nationalism sweeping the preindustrial world") in order to understand the anachronism of the 1947 Statute or the chief determinants of the rebellion? Did some iron law of history dictate that the Algerian revolution start on November 1, 1954, or were there political options which, if seriously pursued, might have altered the course of events? Speculation on historical might-have-beens are, of course, risky and generally fruitless endeavors, but can be justified in this instance in that such assessments were being made in postwar France; and to evaluate their quality we too must attempt an interpretation of the social reality of Algeria—as it was and as it might have been. On the basis of their hopes and fears, men in France read differently—and often falsely—the evidence of events in Algeria. But what exactly did this evidence say? That Algerian independence from France was inevitable? That it must occur through an armed uprising costing the lives of perhaps one Algerian in thirty? Or that it was inevitable only after the paltriness of the Georges Clemenceau reforms (1919), or after the failure of the Blum-Viollette reform (1936), or after the Nazi Occupation of France, or after the disappointing terms of the Algerian Statute of 1947 were set, or after their even more disappointing sabotage beginning in the spring of 1948? When, in other words, were important political options closed, leaving the day to revolt?

Certainly all things were not possible in Algeria. The French presence in North Africa had come to impose definite limitations on France's political options. Thus, the poverty of Algeria and the weakness of French capitalism there presented serious obstacles to the incorporation of the three North African departments (as the Third Republic had come to call them) into France as much as two decades before a Muslim elite issued serious nationalist appeals. Similarly, the misery of the country and the weight of a settler community numbering some 10 percent of the entire population had restricted the development of a Frenchified Muslim bourgeoisie, suggesting that an eventual political confrontation might well take the form of a peasant insurrection. In retrospect, it appears that these developments—as forces of history—began to circumscribe political action thirty to forty years before the uprising actually began. Yet this is not to say that since the early years of this century a revolution in Algeria was inevitable. Later factors, political as well as economic, international as well as local, obviously were of crucial importance. Thus, if with hindsight we can say with some certainty that by the end of World War II no political artistry could have saved French sovereignty in Algeria (and this for international as well as local reasons), it was some time later—perhaps with the beginning of the rigged elections in 1948—that it became likely this separation would occur violently.

Whatever the limitations placed on them by the forces of history, the leaders of Fourth Republic France nevertheless had a succession of policy alternatives open to them in the face of the growing colonial crises in Indochina and Algeria. The purpose here is to lay out what now seem to have been the objective possibilities for French policy in the period after 1945. To do this requires beginning the historical review much earlier, of course, for by 1945, many of the political, and especially economic, factors decisive to the outbreak and eventual success of the revolution were already in place. The intent, then, is to weigh the ambitions of French policy against the reality of conditions in Algeria.

The basic point is this: at some point shortly after the turn of the twentieth century (it becomes apparent in retrospect) France proved unable economically and socially to make Algeria its own. A large native mass, its traditional social structure fragmenting, the modern French system unable to incorporate it, Algeria became available for radical political mobilization. The root failure was economic: Algeria was too poor and French capitalism too weak for integration to succeed. But a large settler population, whose presence was without parallel elsewhere in the empire, exacerbated the problem. The impoverishment and decline of the Muslim community was the necessary consequence of a weak economic system whose benefits flowed primarily to European immigrants and whose structure set the stage for racial confrontation.

On one point at least there seems agreement: at the time of the revolution, the Muslim Algerians were a desperately poor people. Statistics on their production of sheep and grain (principally hard wheat and barley), the chief indicators of the economic well-being of the Muslim sector, reflect a steady and dramatic decline since the coming of the French. Although colonialism displaced the Muslims from the better lands, the area under cultivation by the indigenous population apparently remained relatively stationary through the conversion of poorer tracts to exploitation. Remarkably, production does not seem to have fallen greatly either, except for a gradual interwar decline not reversed until the late 1940's. What is indicative of Muslim privation is the downward plunge of production measured on a per capita basis, as an Algerian birth rate of 2.8 percent (as high as any in the world at the time) cracked the traditional economic base. After World War I, Muslim grain production on a per capita basis fell to about half of what it had been on the average previously, and by still more if comparison is made with the late nineteenth century. For the decade before 1952, output was under 200 kilograms per person, seed and food for livestock included. The decline in sheep was even more spectacular: herds estimated generally at 7.5 to 8.5 million head before World War I fell to between 5 and 6 million thereafter. In 1877, it is estimated there were 3.97 sheep per Muslim; by the time of the revolution, there were only .8 sheep per Algerian Muslim.[9]

Nor were the Muslims able to compensate for this contraction of their staples by diversification of their agricultural base. In 1914, the eminent historian C. R. Ageron notes, Muslim land given over to the cultivation of food and industrial goods other than grain amounted to 11.6% of all land used. I have been

9. Statistical estimates do vary, but the same general pattern is everywhere evident. See Charles Robert Ageron, *Les Algériens musulmans et la France, 1871–1919*, two vols. (Presses Universitaires de France, Paris, 1968), Chapter 29; André Nouschi, *La Naissance du nationalisme algérien* (Editions de Minuit, Paris, 1962), *passim;* and Raymond Barbé, "La Question de la terre en Algérie," and "Les Classes sociales en Algérie," in the June 1955 and September 1959 issues of *Economie et Politique*.

unable to locate statistics on Muslim agricultural production in goods other than food grains for the period after 1914; but the aggregate (Muslim and European) figures for Algeria show a gradual rise until the late 1920's for those goods traditionally grown by the Muslims (olives, dates, tobacco) followed by a sharper decline subsequently. Figures for 1954 put Muslim land used for the production of goods other than grains and orchards at about 10 percent of all land used. From the figures available, it is thus possible to conclude that the diversification of agriculture constituted the base for a small number of Muslim landowners to move from a subsistence to a market economy, but that the trend meant nothing to the great bulk of the rural population.[10]

In the face of the declining per capita productivity of the traditional sector, the Muslim was saved from starvation by his inclusion in what is called the modern European sector of the economy. While labor statistics are difficult to obtain and compare, they are more accurate for the modern than for the traditional sector. Out of 2,142,500 Muslim men listed as active in the census of 1954 (including urban unemployed), 299,000 appear as employees (for the most part workers) in the cities. Another 112,000 are listed in the permanent agricultural work force, though this is probably undercounted 20 to 30 percent to avoid social security payments. Similarly, from the size of their holdings we may assume that 25,000 Muslim landowners produced for the market, while perhaps 9,000 Muslim businessmen (those employing salaried labor) had entered into the modern sector. The occupational census does not take into account the some 275,000 Algerians who had left the country to find work in France. These men nonetheless must be considered basic to Muslim survival, since it was commonly agreed (as stated by Prime Minister Edgar Faure) that their heavy remittances to Algeria sustained 1.5 million people. In all, then, nearly one-third of the Muslim male

10. Ageron, *Les Algériens musulmans,* pp. 797–799. Ageron does not include soft wheat, although this accounted for about 3 percent of Muslim grain production before World War I and was not used for consumption but as a cash crop. *Annuaire statistique* for the years 1925, 1936, and 1939 give the aggregate figures, while Nouschi, *La Naissance du nationalisme algérien,* pp. 116–117, shows those crops of particular importance to the Muslims. Figures on Algeria at the time of the revolution may be found in *Perspectives décennales de développement économique de l'Algérie,* Ministre de l'Algérie (Imprimerie Officielle, Algiers, 1958), p. 173.

labor force was directly concerned with its livelihood within the
European sector of the economy.[11]

Yet, it seems clear that in itself inclusion in the modern sector
did not guarantee even relative economic security since, in nearly
every case, the Muslims were "last hired, first fired," and were
forced by the logic of the situation into the most menial jobs.
Moreover, it is not at all apparent to what extent incorporation
into the European economy was keeping pace with the growing
poverty of the masses on the other side of the economic divide—
in the countryside, part-time and seasonal workers, share-
croppers, and owners of handkerchief plots; in the cities, the
small shopkeepers and artisans, and the officially recognized
unemployed (one-fourth of the active male urban population).
Theirs was not to be a revolution of rising expectations.

On the surface, it is not evident from these figures why the
European presence was not an asset to the Muslim population.
Would not things have been worse had they not been there while
the demographic rate advanced at its high rate? Indeed, however
much French leaders and theorists may have different opinions
among themselves, virtually all of them concluded that the Muslim's problem was his inability to convert to economic modernity
or that the problem grew from the lack of incentive for the
modern European sector to integrate the native mass into it. The
result, in conceptual terms, was to separate the two worlds of
Algeria, to deny the extent to which the Muslim problem lay in
the character of the French presence, and to insist instead that the
primary shortcoming of French rule was not its *domination* but its
neglect of the Muslim population. In other words, the French
could have an easy conscience about Algeria and argue, seemingly in good faith, that the Muslim community would surely
benefit from a genuine effort on the part of Paris to pursue its
"civilizing mission" in North Africa. For the sake of the local

11. *Tableaux de l'économie algérienne,* published by the Office of the Governor
General, Algiers, 1960. See also, R. Barbé, "Les Classes sociales en Algérie, II,"
Economie et Politique, October 1959, for a discussion of the Muslim shopkeepers;
Alain Savary, *Nationalisme algérien et grandeur française* (Plon, Paris, 1960), p. 12,
for a breakdown of Muslim landholding; and Andrée Michel, *Les Travailleurs
algériens en France* (Centre National de la Recherche Scientifique, Paris, 1955), p.
11, puts the number at 186,500 in what is surely an underestimate, since it counts
only those legally in residence in France.

population, then, French sovereignty should not be ended in Algeria but reinvigorated. The terms of this reasoning require closer analysis.

Those who concerned themselves with the Muslim aspect of the dilemma singled out patterns of traditional mental, social, and economic life for consideration. Writing as late as 1962, the French historian Robert Aron sought to locate the Muslim distance from European ways in the former's manner of thinking: they lack "the taste for order and clarity that we have inherited [from Descartes]. . . . They do not know how to reason and argue like us . . . the true nature of Muslim thought reappears—more emotional and sentimental than dialectical and logical."[12] Aron is only echoing here in academic parlance the popular notion of Muslim fatalism and fanaticism, racist stereotypes of common currency among the French of North Africa. In a like manner, the leading economic historian of Algeria during the interwar period had deplored Muslim work habits, "their idleness and nonchalance as soon as the daily needs are met."[13] In a more sophisticated vein, the well-known ethnologist Germaine Tillion argued after the revolution began that the elimination of disease under the French had combined with the customs of an "archaic" and "unadapted" people to permit a ruinous demographic explosion. Unable either to change or to support this heavily mounting burden, the traditional economic base cracked. According to Tillion, the suffering of the Algerian people was simply one aspect of a world-wide process of cultural trauma:

Their misfortune was to find themselves in the impact zone of the modern biological revolution before having attained the level of life and culture which I propose to call the "level of self-protection." And it is here, in my estimation, that our responsibility enters. Responsibility and not culpability, since the present misfortune of Algeria was very likely unavoidable—in the sense that henceforth it is impossible to spare an archaic people all contact with this prodigious monster which is Planetary Civilization and in the measure that this contact is fatal to those unprepared peoples who undergo it.[14]

12. Robert Aron, *Les Origines de la Guerre d'Algérie,* pp. 11–12.
13. Victor Demontès, *Renseignements sur l'Algérie économique* (Office du Gouvernement Générale de l'Algérie, Algiers, 1922), p. 135.
14. Germaine Tillion, *L'Algérie en 1957* (Editions de Minuit, Paris, 1957), pp. 67–68. See especially Chapters 3 and 4.

Probably no theorist in France was cited to explain the Muslim predicament more frequently than Germaine Tillion. Still another way to hold the Muslims responsible for their failure to progress was to indict their system of land tenure, where ownership by extended families allegedly undercut the spirit of individual initiative and enterprise which alone could change these relatively unproductive fields into modern economic units. This "agrarian communism," as the settlers in the nineteenth century like to call it, was hopelessly recalcitrant, or so they insisted, to economic modernization.[15]

Taking another tack, economic historians might argue that it was less for reasons intrinsic to the Muslim life style than for characteristics peculiar to the European sector that local traditional practices were not abolished. According to established models of dual economies, for example, a dynamic industrial system should vitalize a rural area in contact with it through its demand for labor, markets, and cheaper and more plentiful food. In Algeria, however, French settlers, by virtue of their large, capital-intensive farms, had usurped agricultural trade with France from the Muslims. Algeria had not two economic sectors but three, and the third was left in its millenary slumber superfluous to the needs of modern growth. To be sure, this slumber had to be disturbed in order to acquire the best third of the cultivable land in Algeria for the European and to recruit a small native labor force. But it was demographic growth, not the reduction of cultivable land for Muslim use, which weighed most heavily in accounting for Muslim pauperization. As for the exploitation of a Muslim work force, it had eased, not increased, the economic plight of the community. Were one to fault French capitalism it should not be, as readers of the *Communist Manifesto* might believe, for its strength but rather for its weakness. The tragedy, that is, lay not so much in Muslim submission to the capitalist system as in the inability of the Europeans thereby to bring them to modernity. Considered on the balance, this position held that the fault of the French was not so much to *exploit*

15. The most familiar attack on Muslim family structure singled out the role of women. But the economic backwardness of the extended family was the second most popular theme of discussion. See, for example, Victor Demontès, *L'Algérie agricole* (Librairie Larose, Paris, 1930), Chapter 8.

as to *neglect* the traditional system after upsetting its equilibrium. However important the European sector had eventually come to be for Muslim survival in terms of the limited number of employment opportunities it provided, as far as the economic interests of French capitalism were concerned, the Muslims could be left to get along as best they might, more a nuisance for their land holdings, pilfering, and sporadic insubordination than as an asset to the work force.

To sum up the attitudes of the heterogeneous group whose ideas in one form or another dominated the French interpretation of the Algerian problem, the sins of France in Algeria were more those of omission than those of commission. Like the privileged the world over, the French either denied that their prosperity depended on the subordination of the Muslim people, or, even more self-righteously, maintained that their wealth alone could rescue the Muslim from his backwardness. At great effort to himself, the settler had built new cities, roads, schools, and hospitals, and had brought new methods of farming to the country. Perhaps he should have been more generous in associating the Muslim with these benefits; but the misery of the native population would have been greater still had he not come. Consider Egypt. How well had the British done? And what could Gamal Abdel Nasser really promise? As Resident Minister Lacoste, a Socialist, put it before the National Assembly (in a speech soliciting votes to increase the legal powers of repression in Algeria in 1956):

There is not a Frenchman who is willing to see France chased from a land where she implanted herself by the debatable right of arms, but where she has conquered by the undebatable right of a civilizing work made of humanity and generosity. (Applause from the left to the extreme right.) ... The Algerian fellah would have known nothing of liberty and he would have been confronted by an infinitely more tragic misery had Algeria not been integrated into the French community.[16]

In a word, the French were innocent, and it is perhaps no coincidence that the leading exponent in our own day of the politics of innocence should have been a son of Algeria, Albert Camus. Camus' writings are a good illustration of this tendency to

16. *Journal officiel,* March 12, 1956, p. 852.

divide in theory what the settlers tried so assiduously to divide in fact: the two worlds of Algeria. To be sure, Camus was a liberal, appalled by the plight of the Muslim people. But he consistently addressed his fellow settlers as though they should be Good Samaritans, never suggesting that they were responsible (in the sense of being historically linked) for the misery of the 90 percent of the Algerian population which was Muslim.[17] And as we have seen, this view was shared by most Frenchmen who had tried to conceptualize the problem of Muslim impoverishment in colonial Algeria.

Yet, if this theory of European neglect scores points against a too rapid Marxist analysis which might hold capitalist exploitation responsible for the Muslim plight, does it account for all the evidence?[18] Or are there not important indications that French policy in Algeria consciously prevented the modernization of the Muslim sector? Suppose the inability of the traditional sector to modernize was due to more than its own hidebound "premarket mentality" and all which that suggests, or to the strictly economic disinterest of the modern sector for the Muslim population. Suppose instead it was the result of a policy at times overt, at times covert, to exclude these people from the privileges monopolized by the Europeans. To be sure, the basic weakness of the French system played a role in determining such a policy, while the inherent disabilities of the traditional sector allowed it to stand unchallenged. But unlike the word "neglect," which suggests the French simply turned their backs to concern themselves with their own affairs, the word "exclusion" insists upon the element

17. See, for example, Camus' "Misère de la Kabylie" (1939) reprinted in *Actuelles, III: chroniques algériennes* (Gallimard, Paris, 1958). History, according to Camus, has no apparent logic: it is as "absurd" as the universe he first recounts confronting in *The Plague* (1947). Hence no society is ever "guilty" as he declares in regard to the French in Algeria in his 1958 Introduction to *Actuelles, III*. And in *The Fall* (1958) he mocks the spirit of self-condemnation. Camus' ethics of political innocence (*The Rebel, The Just Assassins*) is another matter altogether, although one which was even more important in allowing him to reproach the Algerian revolution for its violent methods.

18. See, for example, Claude Bourdet, "Les Maîtres de l'Afrique du Nord," *Les Temps Modernes*, June 1952; Charles Henri Favrod, *Le FLN et l'Algérie* (Plon, Paris, 1962); Jean-Paul Sartre, "Le Colonialisme est un système," *Situations*, V (Gallimard, Paris, 1964); and Marcel Egrétaud, *Réalité de la nation algérienne* (Editions Sociales, Paris, 1961).

of concerned attention and determined action needed to keep the Muslim society at bay.

A colony won by arms over a people of a totally different culture is maintained by arms until the day when the conquerors can assure their predominance by some other means. The crux of the problem of Muslim impoverishment lay simultaneously in the weakness and the strength of the French economic structure in Algeria: in their strength, the French controlled the political heights and so could parry threats to their sovereignty; but in their weakness, the French did not dare to help the Muslims or to let them organize to help themselves. Nor was the question only economic; ultimately it may be one of racial numbers—as it may also be elsewhere: the Union of South Africa has a much stronger economic base than the French ever did in Algeria, yet never has felt secure enough to move beyond a politics of force toward the native community, and the same basic problem bedevils the Israelis today in the face of the number of Palestinian refugees relative to the Jewish population. As we shall see, moreover, there are good indications that a somewhat more successful modern sector in Algeria would have absorbed *even fewer* Muslims than it did. Less favored than South Africa materially, the French of Algeria had neither the economic nor the demographic strength to absorb the local population. How could the logic of this system be anything other than racist?

There has been a good deal of nonsense written about how purely through the veins of Republican France ran the blood of colonial assimilation. As the story goes, assimilation—the "France of one hundred million Frenchmen," the idea of a "civilizing mission" based on a document of universal import, the Declaration of the Rights of Man—was color blind. But the intention of the Third Republic in Algeria, it might be recalled, was to people the land with Frenchmen, and this did not mean acculturation of the Muslim inhabitants. Rigorously excluded, then, from the concessions of land, the grants of money, and the credit facilities were not only the natives, but also non-naturalized Europeans and naturalized Jews. In practice, the promise of assimilation actually worked as a barrier to deny Muslims their basic civil rights. Since they were not citizens, they were not guaranteed the rights and immunities accorded Frenchmen. But since the alleged ambition was assimilation, the Muslims were not accorded equal status under their own Quranic law either. However much the people of metropolitan France may have thought of assimilation as a bridge to political liberty, in reality it functioned as a barrier.

It is in matters of land and labor that the self-interested domination of the European settlers is probably best seen developing. With the *sénatus-consulte* of 1863, Napoleon III had tried to halt the unbridled acquisition of Muslim land being carried out by the arbitrary exercise of French title to most land in Algeria allegedly inherited from the Turkish dey. The emperor's idea was at once to open Muslim land to colonial acquisition but at the same time to preserve native interests and to facilitate their assimilation to the French system by submitting them to the French form of land tenure. In this fashion, Napoleon would create a Muslim peasantry in the European manner to serve as the bulwark of the French order in Algeria, just as such a base was serving him in metropolitan France. The Law of 1863 provided, therefore, for the disaggregation of the tribes through the division of their communal lands and their settlement into smaller divisions called douars. As the minister for Algeria put it in 1858, "Our goal must be to develop individual initiative and to substitute responsibility, property, and taxation for the cohesion of the tribe in order effectively to prepare the populations to come under civil authority."[19]

As the Arab bureaus charged with surveying the land and recording individual property titles recognized immediately, however, the implementation of the law of 1863 would not encourage the growth of a Frenchified native peasantry but would instead allow the settlers to insinuate themselves still more onto Muslim land. Hence they delayed, meanwhile dividing communal lands into douars but neglecting to record individual titles (to the anger of the settlers). Since title to property could not be transferred nor liens upon it be secured before all tribal property had been individualized, settlers were forced to depend upon state land grants, and the Muslims' extended family system (as opposed to their tribal structure) was left intact.

19. Ageron, *Les Algériens musulmans*, p. 38. On this period see also John Ruedy, *Land Policy in Colonial Algeria* (University of California Press, Los Angeles, 1967).

The creation of the Third Republic and the simultaneous defeat of the Mokrani rebellion in eastern Algeria in 1871 sounded the victory of colonization in its struggle to obtain unhindered access to the land. First, the French punished the Muslims by sequestering some 450,000 hectares of land that was chosen especially for use by settlers and by ordering payment of a heavy indemnity to be used in part to facilitate European immigration.[20] Subsequently, laws were passed in Paris with the express purpose of promoting settlement by making possible private transfers of land. The Law of 1873 (as clarified and amplified by the Law of 1887) provided for the sale by individual Muslims not only of their portion of tribal lands (*arch*) but also of their portion of land held by their extended family (*melk*). Indeed, the decision by one member of a group holding communal property to sell his share could force the sale of the entire parcel. Court and parliamentary decisions checked the worst abuses of this system in the 1890's, but not before the social as well as the economic structure of the Muslim community had in many places been severely shaken.[21]

Estimates place the amount of arable land in northern Algeria at from 5,860,000 to 6,765,000 hectares out of a total surface of 21,000,000 hectares.[22] Climatic and soil conditions are such that only 600,000 hectares were considered truly good land during the colonial regime. During the first twenty years of the Third Republic, the settlers obtained 577,000 hectares from the state and 378,000 hectares by private purchases to add to what they already owned. By 1900, Europeans held 1.7 million hectares; by 1917, 2.3 million; by 1940, 2.7 million.[23] If we can account for the discrepancies in the reports of arable land by data on the extension of irrigation, then since World War I, colonists have held one-third of the cultivable land in Algeria. The importance of

20. Peyerimhoff, *Enquête sur les résultats de la colonisation officielle*, pp. 177–178; Ageron, *Les Algériens musulmans*, Chapter 1.

21. Ageron, *Les Algériens musulmans*, Chapter 4.

22. Northern Algeria comprises the coastal Tell and the plateau and mountain land behind it. Southern Algeria, for the most part identical with the Sahara, is more than sixteen times its size. For the low estimate of arable land, see Ageron, *Les Algériens musulmans*, p. 769; for the high estimate, Barbé in *Economie et Politique*, September 1955, p. 13.

23. Ageron, *Les Algériens musulmans*, p. 101; Barbé, *Economie et Politique*, September 1955.

these holdings depends as much on their quality as on their extent. By the state claiming for itself the former domains of the Turkish dey, and by sequester, expropriation under the right of eminent domain to expand the so-called "perimeters of colonization," and private purchase, the European community had acquired the best land in terms of climate, soil, irrigability, and access routes.

On the domains left to the Muslims, the French system proved hostile to improvement. Agricultural credit facilities—the Caisse algérienne de Crédit agricole mutuel—were heavily oriented toward the European sector, claiming that most Muslims did not possess the proper credentials (in the form of mortgageable land titles, for example) to participate. While statistical reports vary widely as to the sums distributed in short term and equipment loans, they all agree that approximately 90 percent of the credits granted went to 3 percent of the owners, the ones who were European.[24] For the Muslim there was usury—rates of 50 to 60 percent annually were not uncommon—and reliance on a special financial organization, the Sociétés Indigènes de Prévoyance (SIP). Those Muslims who wished to belong subscribed a certain amount and, in turn, could draw upon the SIP when the need for credits arose. Predictably, the record of this organization was distinctly poor. Credits were not alloted either generously or ambitiously; efforts to increase its financial base through obligatory subscriptions were blocked, and schemes to provide other forms of protection—for example, through the construction of grain silos (*mukrama*), a traditional Algerian form of moderating the hardships of bad harvests—were neglected.[25] As Ageron sums it up: "In the end the SIP had not put an end to famine or to usury and had played only a minimal role in the improvement of the native economy. The annual handful of loans brought no well-being to the fellah's agriculture. It had mainly served the Administration to fight famines, to make advances, to distribute charity without it costing anything to the colonial budget."[26] Following World War II, it is true, the system of agricultural

24. Favrod, *Le FLN et l'Algérie*, p. 192; Savary, *Nationalisme algérien*, p. 14.

25. For some unintentionally illuminating remarks by local officials, see Robert Aron, *Les Origines de la Guerre d'Algérie*, pp. 197ff.

26. Ageron, *Les Algériens musulmans*, p. 871.

credits, and especially agricultural instruction with teams of experts, improved noticeably. By this time, however, the situation had long been critical, and despite the dedicated effort of those who worked for these programs, the peasant base for revolution was not significantly reduced.

Not only did the French fail to provide capital credit to the Muslims, but they took a part of the funds available to this community in the form of high taxes. Conveniently renouncing one aspect of their assimilationist program, the French maintained and extended the Turkish tradition of direct taxation of the local population, the *impôts arabes,* in addition to submitting the Muslims to the form of taxation current in the European sector. Ageron estimates that until 1919, when these special taxes were cancelled, the Muslim community had been paying some 60 percent of the various budgets in Algeria. On the local level, in settler-controlled villages (called *communes de plein exercice,* in reference to their "full exercise" of French political ways), this percentage reached its highest level, sometimes covering 80 percent of municipal expenses. In return, the Muslims received precious little indeed. Ageron calculates that in 1918, the total spent on charitable houses, hospitals, schools, justice, and religion for the Muslim population amounted to 3.1 percent of the Algerian budget.[27] The improvements the French liked to boast their presence brought to Algeria were clearly not funded by their charity.

Discrimination against the Muslim was far more pervasive than the question of land, although this was perhaps the basic factor working to keep the two communities apart. The main avenue into the world of the bourgeoisie in France had always been through education. Under the Third Republic, the myth of the "career open to talents" had a place of honor. In Algeria, however, the French education program for Muslims was most notable by its absence. A review of the record shows that this was far from neglect on the Europeans' part, but was the consequence of a consistent and determined effort not to open up the modern economic structure to Muslim penetration through the pride of the Third Republic, the schoolroom. On different occasions, the

27. Ageron, *Les Algériens musulmans,* pp. 1233–1235.

French of Algeria diverted, vetoed, even refused funds from Paris intended for Muslim education. After closing schools specifically designed for Muslim children under the Second Empire through the pretext of assimilating them to the French system, local authorities in Algeria worked to disaffect the Muslims from the new mixed schools where they were made available. Special vocational schools likewise stagnated for lack of funds. The rudimentary Muslim education system which survived the loss of revenue lands (*habous*) belonging to the mosques, was alternately tolerated for the poor quality of its instruction, harassed in order to prevent the growth of fanaticism, or, less often, upgraded under the pressures of staffing the French administrative apparatus with competent Arabists. Statistics sum up the results: in 1892, 1.73 percent of Muslims of primary school age were being educated in the French manner; by 1954, the number of Muslims being educated in the fashion of first class citizens in the *primary* schools of Algeria was 3.46 percent of the school age population.[28] Unable to maintain themselves in the traditional manner, yet unable to integrate themselves into the European system, the Muslim's plight was a desperate one and gradually worsening.

As one might expect, the French could maintain such a system only by strictly monopolizing political power. To be sure, the system had its weak points as a result of liberal influence from the metropole. But in the early years this was not readily apparent. Fractured by the French landing (1830), the defeat of Abd al-Qadir (1847), and the imposition of Arab bureaus, tribal cohesion in Algeria was finally undermined by the *sénatus-consulte* of 1863 which, as we have seen, broke the tribes into smaller settlements and distributed community property among them. Political reorganization remained strictly in French hands. Three sorts of local administration were set up, depending on the number of Eu-

28. Statistics for the early years may be found in Favrod, *Le FLN et l'Algérie*, p. 178, and in Ageron, *Les Algériens musulmans*, Chapter 12. For the period just prior to the Revolution see Raymond Aron, *L'Algérie et la République* (Plon, Paris, 1958), pp. 18ff; and *Notes et Etudes Documentaires*, number 1215. Aron reports that 16.5 percent of those Muslims of primary school age attended classes in 1954, but he neglects to mention that students in Algeria were placed on one of two tracks. While only 5 percent of the European children were tracked to finish their education with primary schooling, 79 percent of the Muslims were so handled.

ropeans in the area. Where few were present, the French established so-called *communes indigènes* under military command. These were for the most part located far to the south and were of no political significance. Most Muslims fell under the jurisdiction of a *commune mixte*, where an appointed administrator (under the Second Empire, a military officer) was in charge, acting with a municipal council whose European members were elected (under the Third Republic) and whose Muslim members were appointed. From the early days of the Third Republic, however, most Europeans lived in the metropolitan manner in regularly constituted *communes de plein exercice* alongside (by 1911) over a quarter of the Muslim population. Here both Muslims and French elected a municipal council whose European members in turn selected a mayor. However, only a restricted list of Muslims could vote and this for at best one-third (in certain periods one-fourth) of the council seats. Despite the greater representation of the Muslims in these latter towns, the relatively unchecked power of the settlers there made these jurisdictions the most difficult for the Muslims to live in.[29]

Above the local level, Algeria was divided into districts (*arrondissements*) which in turn formed three departments (each much larger than its metropolitan equivalent), headed by prefects. Final authority lay with the governor general, who was linked to Paris through the minister of the interior. Yet Algeria was far more decentralized than this schema may suggest. From 1881 to 1896, a system of "direct attachments" had deprived local authorities of much of their power, while the eight ministries in Paris decided Algerian questions. But after 1896, power for the most part devolved again to the governor general and those beside him. Prefects, usually of settler origin, were assisted in their tasks by elected councils general composed unequally of Europeans (four-fifths) and Muslims (who were appointed until 1908, then elected by a restricted college of only 5,000 until 1919). After 1898, Algeria also had limited financial autonomy. Elected financial delegations were composed of three groups: first, Muslim (selected from a restricted electoral college), second, the French farmers, third, the urban Frenchmen paying personal taxes; the

29. Confer, *France and Algeria: The Problem of Civil and Political Reform, 1870–1920, passim;* and Ageron, *Les Algériens musulmans,* Chapters 6 and 23.

delegations could oversee the local budget and had substantial prestige as a rudimentary sort of Algerian Assembly. In addition, a superior council composed of government officials and delegates elected from the councils general and the financial delegations sat beside the governor general. Finally, there were the various staffs responsible to the governor general, recruited for the most part from among the French of Algeria. Under the Third Republic, the settlers had as well the right to three senators and from six to ten deputies to the parliament in Paris. From this vantage point in France, and with the aid of well-financed lobbies, they were able to put pressure on the one man they could not always control in Algeria, the governor general.[30]

In short, during the first three decades of the Third Republic, the settlers managed to establish a political structure so supple that, except for the most determined opposition, it could effectively: (1) call for support from Paris when it was needed; (2) isolate itself from the pressures of Paris when it seemed necessary; (3) insure the political subordination of the Muslim community. Certainly it had to deal with troublesome official investigations (Jules Ferry from 1891–1893), reformist governor generals (Jules Martin Cambon in the 1890's, Yves Chatigneau in the 1940's), determined prime ministers (Georges Clemenceau in 1919), and the threat of decree power held by the prime minister (Léon Blum in 1936). But it inevitably recovered its stability until the combined assault of the Algerian revolutionaries and Charles de Gaulle swept it away.

Not only tribal, but especially religious, leaders had wielded political power in Algeria before the French arrival. In the absence of central or even feudal authorities, holy men—*marabouts*—through their possession of mystical power (*baraka*) had come to act as judges, legislators, and leaders. Islamic brotherhoods (*tariqa*), sometimes working with *marabouts* or growing from them, constituted fraternities whose allegiances bridged not only tribes, but even distant regions of North Africa. Abd al-Qadir, for example, was a leader (*moqaddem*) of the Quadriya religious

30. Herbert Liebesny, *The Government of French North Africa* (University of Pennsylvania Press, Philadelphia, 1943). On informal political arrangements, see A. S. Kanya-Forstner, "The French 'Colonial Party': Its Composition, Aims, and Influence," *Historical Journal,* March 1971.

brotherhood, and there were other fraternities that were involved in the massive uprising under Mokrani in 1871. While the French were ultimately able to use these organizations to their own ends, they did not hesitate to eliminate those resisting their rule. At such times, the French seized all revenue lands belonging to the mosques, and in one stroke reduced Islam—at least for a time—to dependence on the French state. So also were the clergy named, salaried, supervised, and even arranged in hierarchy; religious education declined drastically; pilgrimages to Mecca were discouraged; religious property was allowed to deteriorate (or, as in the case of the principal mosques of Algiers and Constantine, was transformed into Catholic property); and a host of regulations appeared to insure the political sterilization of the clergy. Ironically, the separation of church and state so assiduously championed in France never found much support in Algeria (except among those who hoped to damage Islam even more thereby).

The French completed their monopoly of power in Algeria by a system of justice which, if it respected Muslim law in regard to what was called personal status (for example, in marriage and inheritance), exercised French law in regard to most questions of criminality and property (all instances in which one party was French). In addition, a series of laws particular to Muslims were finally codified in 1881. These special regulations, the *indigénat*, included an internal passport system, forced labor, and penalties for acts or remarks prejudicial to French sovereignty or to the authority of public officials.[31] Those who maintain that French concepts of universalism prevented them from being realistic about adjusting to the end of empire after World War II might well consider that similar doctrines never seemed to inhibit a realistic answer to the problems of the expansion of this empire.

So Napoleon III's dream of a Muslim peasantry exploiting the land in the French manner failed. On the one hand, European purchases and expropriations had dispossessed many, yet on the other, virtually no measures were taken to promote Muslim advancement. In itself the land issue need not have meant the Muslim's economic ruin if circumstances had been right so that he

31. Ageron, *Les Algériens musulmans,* Chapters 7 and 25 and pp. 165–175.

could have achieved a transformation in his life style never imagined by Napoleon. The great Russian Minister Pëtr Arkadevich Stolypin, for example, had broken up the land of the *mir,* thinking thereby to create a conservative peasant strata but quite aware of the landless proletariat which would thereby be formed. Why in Algeria, then, could the more fortunate of the Muslims not buy out their fellows, just as the Europeans were doing, with those who were dispossessed going to work on the large farms created by this process of concentration or moving on to work in the cities?

Despite the severe restrictions on Muslim advancement which, as we have seen, ranged from lack of credit facilities to absence of opportunities for education, the process of incorporation was apparently beginning to occur in Algeria after the turn of the century. The subject awaits its economic historian, but a trend seems evident in terms of the formation of a native middle peasantry producing for the market (25,000 families perhaps) and a permanent agricultural proletariat, in addition to an increasing Muslim work force both in the cities of Algeria and in metropolitan France. As we have already seen, however, an equally modern and more miserable group was also forming, one that combined the urban unemployed, the *meskine* or rural workless, the sharecropper, the migrant laborer.

Yet if the answer would seem to be stronger economic activity by France in Algeria, there is good reason to doubt this would have been successful, at least in the short term. That is, *it does not follow that a more powerful capitalist system in Algeria would necessarily have rescued the Muslims from their misery and eased the tensions of racial confrontation there, however much this belief may have appealed to a wide spectrum of opinion under the Fourth Republic.* To pretend the settler could bring salvation to the Muslim was a cruel, if convenient, illusion from which the Republic could not rouse itself. Take, for example, the history of the development of Algeria's most important product during the colonial period, wine. When, after 1863, the phylloxera epidemic began progressively to destroy the vineyards of France, many concluded that Algeria had at last found her economic vocation. Substantial amounts of capital became available to enterprising settlers, a process of vinification was developed to nullify the damage caused by the heat of North

Africa, and during the 1880's wine making was established as the most valuable, the most labor specialized, and the most labor intensive commercial business in Algeria. Initially, however, the benefits derived from wine making were used not to aid the Muslim or to work for the integration of the two communities, but to promote the growth and solidarity of the European community. Campaigns were launched in France and from Algeria, not to make use of the new activity for the assimilation of the natives, but to stimulate the growth of the European colony. Wine had been the mainstay of a small peasantry in France, so officials anticipated that viticulture could provide the foundation for a massive relocation of French growers in North Africa. Since vineyards are labor specialized and labor intensive, particularly at their inception, a permanent agricultural work force of European descent, it was thought, could be recruited to Algeria. Officials encouraged emigration from throughout southern France and a regular steamship service was inaugurated between Oran and Spain by which large numbers of migrant workers arrived each year in Algeria. Those Muslims hired to work in the vineyards found themselves with the lowest of pay and the most menial of jobs, segregated from the Europeans and barred from improving their position.[32]

Significantly, it was not so much this economic expansion in Algeria as economic *crisis* for the wine producers which increasingly associated the Muslims with the vineyards. In 1893, the vineyards in France unexpectedly having recovered through imports of blight resistant plants from California, the first crisis of overproduction occurred. So began the pattern of foreclosures and land concentrations that erased the possibility of establishing in Algeria a small French peasantry based on the vine. At the same time, wages fell, reducing the flow of skilled labor from Europe. Simultaneously, wages and property values increased in metropolitan France with the decline of the epidemic, while the Spanish peseta, for other reasons, was revalued. Setback for the

32. Hildebert Isnard, *La Vigne en Algérie,* two vols. (Editions Ophrys, Gap, 1947), and "La Viticulture algérienne: erreur économique?" *Revue Africaine,* Algiers, 1956. An argument against this interpretation could maintain that it was rational, economically speaking, to hire Europeans for this work since they were better skilled and acculturated to work discipline.

Europeans meant advancement for the Muslims. Slowly the Muslim was upgraded until, by the interwar period, he was indispensable to the vineyards of Algeria. Had wine making been more successful in Algeria, had, for instance, the French vineyards in fact been permanently destroyed as was feared at first, what indication is there that the Muslim community would have been correspondingly advantaged? It had been the weakness, not the strength, of viticulture in Algeria that had secured the Muslims a foothold in the modern economic sector. Such a finding fits poorly with the understanding of Algeria current in Fourth Republic France where it was held, as we have seen, that it was a weak French economic system in Algeria which neglected the Muslim and that the two communities would have been better reconciled if reforms had been instigated to invigorate the area economically.

A stronger capitalist system in Algeria would have been unwilling to employ the Muslims without first having encouraged the influx of as many Europeans as possible to swell its ranks. While the French were not as explicit in their colonization program as the Europeans of South Africa or the Zionists in Palestine —both of whom specifically encouraged immigration by reserving choice economic opportunities for their own kind—the understanding was that Algeria would become French primarily by an infusion of European blood, the rhetoric of assimilation notwithstanding. Thus, the major public-works programs in Algeria meant not the training of Muslims, but the immigration of, in this instance, Italians.[33] Similarly, what gains the Muslims made into the urban work force in the twentieth century seem to have had less to do with the ability of the capitalist system in Algeria to provide for them than with its *inability* to provide competitive wages and thereby draw to North Africa the numbers of Europeans it never ceased to prefer.[34] Suppose, for example, that the tremendous oil and gas reserves of the Sahara had been discovered in the 1920's, when it would have given Algeria a

33. See the passing remarks made by Hélène Weiler, "Peuplement et démographie," in Jean Alazard et al., eds., *Initiation à l'Algérie* (Maisonneuve, Paris, 1957).

34. Savary, *Nationalisme algérien*, p. 24, states that 71 percent of the settlers earned half or less than half of the French national average. Such facts could hardly have stirred much enthusiasm for emigration to North Africa.

considerable economic potential, rather than in the 1950's. Whatever Muslim labor might have become associated with its development, it seems consistent with French practice that the first concerns for distributing its advantages would have been to the reinforcement of European predominance. A stronger economic foundation would have offered the French of Algeria a defense against both the Muslims (through the anticipated immigration of more Europeans) and against Paris (through threat of secession in the manner of South Africa). Undoubtedly, a far more vigorous European economic sector would have absorbed more of the vast labor reservoir in Algeria. But the process would have been slow, with the Muslims relegated to the most menial positions and the Europeans anxious to increase their own numbers.

Such a system in place, one wonders if those metropolitan liberals who so ceaselessly denounced the "stubborn blindness" of the settlers on the subject of reform were not themselves more truly blind. Political freedom and economic mobility were pious daydreams for a land where deep cultural antagonism had come to be compounded by economic conflict. The Muslims had all the grievances of a defeated and despoiled race. Who would guarantee that a new-found ability to organize, debate, and act would not result in the eviction of France from Algeria? What would Muslims do with majorities on municipal councils and councils general? The Europeans were well aware what could be accomplished given such power. The Muslim had not converted (despite the attempts of the church), or naturalized, or—as the settlers feared—surrendered. "When the Muslims protest you become indignant, when they approve you become suspicious, when they are silent you become worried"—such was the famous observation made by one-time Governor General Viollette to the Europeans of Algeria in 1935. Indeed, one searches the historical record in vain for a single instance of a generous gesture by the European community to the Muslims. The settlers combatted without exception every measure by Paris to improve the lot of the Muslim population. Such a system had a self-perpetuating logic. The French had been the first to define the character of the racial relationship in Algeria: a gain by one side was a loss for the other. Subsequently, piecemeal reforms could legitimately be forecast as easily to incite the Muslims to insubordination as to rally them to the French presence. In three-quarters of a century of settler opinion on the Muslim, one finds no metaphor expressed so often as the fear of being "drowned" in the Muslim "tide." *Bougnoules, melons, ratons,*—their world would never be that of the French. "They don't have the same needs as us. . . [that is] what most Europeans think," wrote Jules Roy, a leftist writer of Algerian birth, of their frame of mind. "The Arabs are a dirty race and our error has been to treat them with humanity."[35] As one Secret Army Organization (OAS) booklet put it: "The right of France to stay in Algeria is a solid right. It is that of the builders of cathedrals which is superior to that of the builders of mud huts. The ground belongs to those who work it, not to those who sleep on it."[36]

Such views were especially popular among "the little whites" who inflated their self-importance at the expense of the Muslims. Because of the caste system based on race, "the least official is a king" observed Pierre Nora.[37] Or as Sartre wrote:

But if the Muslim affirms himself in turn as a man, as an equal to the settler? Then the settler is attacked in his being; he feels diminished, devalued: the advancement of the "coons" to the world of men he sees not only in its economic consequences, he abominates it because it means his personal dethronement. In his fury he comes to dream of genocide.[38]

It was no accident that Bab-el-Oued, the working-class district of Algiers that traditionally voted Communist, became the center of OAS activity in Algeria. As one of the movement's defenders put it, "the OAS was born of the Algerian population. . . . What must be understood to grasp its evolution is the extremely deep physical implantation of France in Algeria."[39] It is indicative in this regard that before the Sétif outbreak in 1945, the pattern of community confrontation took the form of political abuses on the

35. Jules Roy, *La Guerre d'Algérie* (Julliard, Paris, 1960).

36. XXX, "Ecrit en prison" (anonymous), *L'Activiste* (Editions Jeanne d'Arc, Paris, 1963), p. 5.

37. Pierre Nora, *Les Français d'Algérie* (Editions de Minuit, Paris, 1960), p. 50. The mocking superiority of the tone of this book contrasts with the sympathy shown in Roy's book.

38. Jean-Paul Sartre, "Une Victoire," *Situations*, V, pp. 85–86.

39. Marc Lauriol in his testimony at General Salan's trial, *Le Procès Salan* (Nouvelles Editions Latines, Paris, 1962), pp. 231–232.

part of the Muslims and racial abuses on the part of the French. So the liberal Governor General Viollette became "Viollette l'arabe," while Chatigneau was called "Sidi Chatigneau."[40]

The great error of metropolitan France was not so much to condone as to deny the racial opposition in Algeria. Writing in 1948, Camus could say:

I sum up here the history of the men of my family who, in addition, being poor and without hatred, have never oppressed nor exploited anyone. But three-fourths of the French of Algeria resemble them and, on condition that one gives them reasons rather than insults, will be ready to admit the need of a more just and free order.[41]

The French left was quite willing to accept such groundless pledges, content to direct its attack at the wealthy settlers and so spare "the little whites" of the country who generally voted left of center. Thus, during his term as minister of the interior, Edouard Depreux, a Socialist, declared before the National Assembly: "[Settlers and Muslims] have quite exactly the same interests. . . . These honest people, these workers . . . who have kept so well their pioneering state of mind and who do not go there to oppress the Muslims but in order to gain their livelihood honestly, love the Muslims as they deserve to be loved by them."[42]

As late as 1955, another prominent Socialist, Christian Pineau, could state: "Alongside the big settlers for whom profit alone matters and for which they are ready to sacrifice anything, there are the French of Algeria who work in conditions often difficult, who are not 'colonialists,' who understand the complaints and the aspirations of the Muslim population."[43]

It was the one Socialist (Mollet) who could have done something about the situation from his position as prime minister who *did* understand the dilemma:

The right wing extremists so often attacked are sometimes recruited—this will surprise you—among the most humble of the Europeans, those whom I will call the 'little whites.' . . . [They have] privileges dangerous for the good accord of the communities. It is they who scorn the Arab or

40. See the reports assembled in Robert Aron, *Les Origines de la Guerre d'Algérie*, Part 2, Chapter 1.
41. Albert Camus, *Actuelles, III*, p. 22.
42. *Journal officiel*, August 23, 1946, p. 3283.
43. *Combat*, July 29, 1955.

the Kabyle, often more cultivated; it is they who are the most opposed to an agreement for fear of losing their little advantages."[44]

Yet Guy Mollet refused to follow this line of thinking when he was in office and could have dealt effectively with settler opinion in Algeria.

Was there a "missed opportunity" in Algeria when Paris might have made these three departments genuinely French? Such a development would have required economic and political policies that were obviously not the order of the day in the first quarter of this century. But only a dogmatist would insist the process was inconceivable. If France, for example, had recruited from Algeria a far larger labor force for industrial work than was the case, and had associated a Muslim elite with the exercise of power locally and nationally, the relationship between these two peoples might have been far different. France traditionally imported very large numbers of industrial workers, and France was a liberal country politically.[45] But Third Republic France had other priorities and, in any case, to this "stalemate society" postponement was a way of life. In the case of Algeria, delay served only to exacerbate the problem.

For it was becoming progressively clear after the turn of the century that the other possible solution favorable to France in Algeria, the triumph there of colonialism, was doomed. The brake in French expansion may be associated with the settlement of the land. From 1872 to 1890, the number of Europeans had doubled from 100,000 to 200,000, and had come to represent better than 40 percent of the non-Muslim population. In absolute figures, their numbers continued slowly to grow until the 1920's when they were more than 230,000. But two decades earlier the decline of the rural population in relation to the urban element had begun. Since the turn of the century, immigration too had fallen, and the census of 1931 confirmed what had been feared

44. Guy Mollet, *Bilan et perspectives socialistes* (Plon, Paris, 1958), p. 55.
45. The conservative base of the Third Republic was guaranteed by a stable peasantry. Factory workers were imported in large numbers; Algerians were not favored in these arrangements, however. See Granotier, *Les Travailleurs immigrés en France*, Chapter 2; L. Muracciole, *L'Emigration algérienne: aspects économiques, sociaux, et juridiques (Ferraris, Algiers, 1950); "L'Immigration en France depuis cent ans,"* *Esprit*, April 1966.

for some time, a decline in absolute numbers of rural Europeans. Between 1936 and 1948, the total European population actually declined, and by 1954, only slightly better than 10 percent of the French, just over 100,000 persons, lived outside the cities.[46]

As the momentum of colonialism declined, so the energy of the native society seemed to accelerate. Since the 1880's, the Europeans had come to realize that the Muslim was not going to die out like the American Indian or the Australian aborigine. The previous decline in native population as a consequence of famine and French repression had reversed. At first the French could lay this to the credit of their civilizing work in North Africa, but fear behind the boast became evident as it became clear that the native society would not only stay many times the size of the French, but that it was growing at a faster rate. The 1931 census established as well that the Muslims had also moved into a decided numerical superiority in the towns.

"In a word, we must be strong enough to survive the injustice of which we will stand condemned in Arab eyes," declared T. R. Bugeaud de la Piconnerie, conqueror of Algeria, in the 1840's. Yet sometime after the turn of the century (it becomes clear in retrospect), colonialism had failed to attain the material or demographic strength to digest Algeria. So the major socioeconomic forces which would come to mark the character of the future revolution began to move into position. In a different century, in a different dress, the French were once again acting out the drama of the *ancien régime*.

46. Once again, figures vary although the general pattern is everywhere the same. For the period before World War I, see Ageron, *Les Algériens musulmans*, pp. 546–548, 551. For later figures, see Barbé, *Economie et Politique*, September 1959. Official statistics for 1954 are in *Tableaux de l'économie algérienne*, p. 22.

5 The Formulation of the Consensus on Algeria

It appears that just as the reforms of 1896 to 1900 were finally assuring a supple political apparatus for Algeria in terms of favoring settler domination there, the developing configuration of social and economic forces in the country was, on the contrary, making such an arrangement patently reactionary. To be sure, compared to the government they had replaced in Algeria in 1830, the French may at first have seemed political virtuosos. The organization of their bureaucracy and the strength of their army easily eclipsed the abilities of the weak Turkish authorities preceding them in Algiers and eventually established the strongest links between the cities and the rural populace that this part of the Maghrib had ever known. But as the serious social and economic problems born of the disintegration of the traditional Muslim system combined with other twentieth-century forces to produce a new breed of Muslim political leadership, the French order faltered. Unable to be democratic in Algeria for reasons we have seen, the French also proved unable to be consistently authoritarian. Hence they failed to institutionalize either of the two forms of rule that have survived the test of twentieth-century mass political participation. Instead, their presence was characterized by a lethal mixture of liberality, which allowed discontent to organize; authoritarianism, which from ignorance and fear failed to satisfy the demands that had been allowed to collect; and neglect, which (true of the pattern familiar to the Third

Republic) was the favored road to pursue where no one position on a problem could be consistently adopted. It was this untenable contradiction, far more than repression alone, that set French rule off from that in South Africa and which explains an important part of the revolution's origin and success. In its clumsy efforts successively to repress, to allay, or, worst of all perhaps, to disregard Muslim hostility, the French system failed to deal effectively with the increasingly conscious and organized native leadership of the interwar period.

Clemenceau's political reforms for Algeria in 1919—which at the moment seemed a terribly bold step—may for a time have shielded the truth. Over the opposition of the French of Algeria, Paris softened the strictures of the *indigénat*, abolished the system of unequal taxation (thereby lowering the Muslim charge by some 50 percent), reduced somewhat the barriers to Muslim naturalization to French citizenship, called for the election rather than the appointment of Muslims to local assemblies other than the *communes de plein exercice*, and substantially increased the number of Muslims eligible to vote.[1] As events were to demonstrate, however, these modifications were less fundamental than they might initially have appeared, serving neither to upset, as the conservatives had warned, nor to reinforce, as the liberals had believed, French control over the country politically. Since few Muslims would willingly abandon their status as subject to Islamic law in order to obtain the benefits of French citizenship, little more use was made of the facilities for naturalization after 1919 than had been made before under the provisions of 1865. In addition, the European community remained clearly dominant on the local level, despite the increased number of Muslims given the vote.[2] Subsequently, the colonists would alternatively blame native unrest on the untoward liberalization measures of 1919, or take shelter behind them as the most progressive steps French

1. Confer, *France and Algeria*, pp. 85–115.
2. By 1936, only 7,818 Muslims had been naturalized. See *Notes et Etudes Documentaires*, number 678 (1947). In the Municipal Councils, Muslim representation did rise, from one-fourth to one-third of the seats, and they could now vote for the mayor. As early as 1920, however, the French annulled the election of the Emir Khaled to the Algiers Municipal Council as a result of his program to abolish second-class citizenship for the Muslims.

sovereignty in Algeria could tolerate, evidence enough of European good faith. The Muslims, for their part, failed to find their prewar grievances satisfied. And, as we have seen, the logic of the economic situation severely limited the likelihood that these political tensions could easily be resolved.

It was during this interwar period, which was characterized by economic antagonism between the two races and by failure to find a genuine political accommodation, that the forces of modern Algerian nationalism began to come to consciousness and to organize. Four quite different groups, sometimes collaborating, sometimes competing, sponsored this development. The first in time and importance owed its consistency through the years, despite its many appellations (successively, ENA, GENA, PPA, MTLD, MNA), to the character of its forceful leader Messali Hadj.[3] In 1926, under the inspiration of the French Communist party, the North African Star (ENA), soon to fall under Messali's leadership, began to work among the Algerian proletariat in France. By early 1929, when the movement was dissolved by government order, Messali was popular enough to draw audiences of over 1,000 when he came to speak, and the ENA had a membership of some 4,000.[4]

Until at least 1933, Communist aid to Messali was indispensable. Party funds underwrote the newspapers of the ENA and the GENA, and the mayors of communist municipalities arranged for social security protection for jobless or ill North Africans in France. In addition, Messali learned the rhetoric of class conflict and the technique of party organization. Unlike the other political elites acting on behalf of Muslim grievances, Mess-

3. Etoile Nord Africaine (ENA), 1926, dissolved in 1929; Glorieuse Etoile Nord Africaine (GENA), 1932, dissolved in 1933 and again in 1937; Parti Populaire Algérien (PPA), 1937, clandestine; Mouvement pour le Triomphe des Libertés Démocratiques (MTLD), 1946, split in 1953–1954; Mouvement National Algérien (MNA), 1955.

4. The following discussion of the Messalistes comes from the Archives of the Prefecture of Policy of the City of Paris, whose agents had infiltrated the nationalist ranks from its earliest days. Messali was quickly recognized as the movement's undisputed leader, a man of charismatic power. Although he worked as a laborer and an itinerant salesman of women's stockings, one report notes, "By hard work, he has become truly cultured, reading voraciously, taking notes, assiduously taking courses at the Sorbonne, the School of Oriental Languages, and the College de France."

ali went directly to the masses. In Paris, this resulted particularly in the organization of North African taxicab drivers, which the Paris police reported made a most effective communications network. At the time of its dissolution, sixteen of the twenty-eight members of the Central Committee of the ENA were simultaneously members of the French Communist party.

Although the French Communist party funded the rebirth of Messali's movement in 1931, the PCF proved less and less able to maintain its control over the North African leader. Stimulated by contact with Tunisian and Moroccan students in Paris and by the arrival in the French capital of certain Algerian reformist religious leaders, Messali directed his followers increasingly toward a brand of Islamic nationalism alien to Marxism. The Communists, for their part, found themselves growing more at odds with Messali ideologically, while politically, obliged to face the mounting threat of Hitler, they moved to reduce their anti-imperialist agitation. Always a violent anti-Semite and leary of the Jews in the PCF, Messali completed his move away from communism in his encounters with the pan-Islamic (and pro-Italian) nationalist Shakib Arslan in Geneva in 1935–1936. While this split between the Communists and Messali undoubtedly appealed to the French interior ministry, Messali nonetheless remained quite alarming, for alone in the late interwar period he championed unequivocally the independence of Algeria.[5]

A second Muslim political movement beginning to emerge in the 1920's recruited its members from among the Frenchified middle classes of the towns, and, more particularly, from among those of this class who served in various local assemblies of Algeria. Called the Fédérations des Elus (later referred to in the singular),[6] the initial importance of the association depended not so much on its numbers as on its position, for education, social and economic interest, and elected position made its members a natural link between the French and Muslim communities. Quite

5. The Police Archives were open only to World War II. They contain two reports of some scope, "Note sur l'activité de l'Etoile Nord Africaine depuis sa création jusqu'au 15 novembre 1934," and a report dated February 4, 1937, to the Haut Comité de la Méditerranée et de l'Afrique du Nord.
6. Although the movement is usually dated as having been founded in Constantine in 1934, a similar group had been organized in Algiers in 1927.

unlike Messali, these middle class *évoulés* looked to France to redeem her pledges to undertake the wholehearted assimilation of her North African departments. To this end, Doctor Bend-jelloul and Ferhat Abbas, as its leaders, built a program that called for administrative and political equality between the French and Muslim populations without the abandonment of the Quranic status of the former.[7] Both their program and their unity fell apart with the shelving of the Blum-Viollette proposals for Algeria in 1938.[8] Thereafter, a minority with Bendjelloul continued to work with the French for assimilation until September 1955 when, after the Philippeville nationalist uprising and repression, they declared themselves in the Declaration of Sixty-One to be partisans of the cause of Algerian independence. Abbas, with a larger following, had reached this conclusion twelve years earlier, in terms spelled out in his Manifesto of the Algerian People (which was presented to the French authorities shortly after the Allied landing in North Africa). Its provisions stated that "Algeria will be constituted as the State of Algeria having its own constitution which will be drawn up by a Constituent Algerian Assembly, elected by universal suffrage of all the inhabitants of Algeria."[9] Ultimately, as we know, this middle class was to become historically irrelevant. The weakness of the French presence economically, combined with the large settler population, worked together seriously to inhibit the development of a strong native class interested in collaborating with the French (which was the case, by way of contrast, with Félix Houphouet-Boigny in the Ivory Coast and elsewhere in French Black Africa). Having failed to create in Algeria a group with whom it could relatively easily negotiate a transfer of power as the pressure of local nationalism increased,

7. Since 1916, this had been the arrangement for Muslims of Senegal in *communes de plein exercice.*

8. This proposal's major provision would have been to admit immediately to French citizenship, without abandoning Quranic status, some 20,000 to 25,000 Muslims, with the number gradually increasing. See *Notes et Etudes Documentaires*, number 678, p. 5.

9. These were the terms of the more outspoken Addendum to the Manifesto, added one month after the publication of the main text, on May 26, 1943. See *Notes et Etudes Documentaires*, number 333.

the French were to find themselves faced with a popular insurrection led by men of the people.[10]

A third Muslim organization, the Ulama Association of Algeria (Association des Oulémas d'Algérie) never acquired the formal characteristics of a party, although its presence throughout Algeria and its substantial nationalist influence was never in doubt. A movement of reformist religious leaders, the Association transmitted into Algeria currents of Sunnite Islamic thought that originated toward the end of the nineteenth century in the Middle East with el-Afghani and his disciple Shaykh Abuh. Under the able leadership of Sheik Abd el-Hamid Bin Badis and his colleagues Tayeb el-Oqbi and Bashir al-Brahimi, the Ulama established a broad educational network that reached outside the towns into the countryside. Simultaneously, they began to publish weekly and monthly reviews, as well as histories of Algeria. Their ambition, to purify and regenerate Islam in the twentieth century, was ostensibly nonpolitical. But their religious enemies were the docile instruments of the French state whose policy for one hundred years had been to encourage the Muslim religion into political quiescence, while their allies in the Middle East had begun to link the purpose of their action to the revival of the entire Muslim world. As early as 1933, the French administration viewed their progress with concern and began to monitor and harass their activities. In 1936, the Ulama acknowledged their political role when they agreed to participate in the First Muslim Congress of Algeria held in June of that year.

A fourth group of significance to the evolution of Algerian nationalism during the period between World War I and World War II was the Algerian Communist party (PCA). In 1924, the French Communists had set up a section of their party in Algeria, but in 1935, the decision to create an Arab Communist party led to the formation of the quasi-independent Algerian Communist party and the substantial Arabization of its hierarchy. Following the directives of the Third International, the party had early begun to speak out for an independent Algeria, and between

10. For a comparison of the style of nationalist uprising in the Ivory Coast, Indochina, and Algeria (as well as India and Indonesia) see Smith "A Comparative Study of French and British Decolonization."

1925 and 1927 the party had opposed strenuously the combined Franco-Spanish repression of the Moroccan leader Abd el-Krim in the Rif War. But by 1937, the menace of Hitler and the obligations of membership in the Popular Front persuaded the party to modify this stand somewhat, just as the pressures of the Cold War and the attitude of its European backers encouraged a more nuanced attitude toward Algerian independence after 1945. In a rapidly polarizing environment, however, such a program could not survive. Although the party claimed to have tripled in size between 1939 and 1946, Muslim nationalism made off with the bulk of its native voters in the elections of June 1946 to the Second Constituent Assembly. Its movement toward a nationalist policy thereafter resulted in the defection of much of its European following in the October 1946 elections to the first legislature of the National Assembly of the Fourth Republic. Nevertheless, by the relative sophistication of its organization and appeals, by its membership in both communities in Algeria (largely through the trade union movement), and by the importance of its international and metropolitan connections, the PCA remained a force with which to reckon.[11]

These movements were almost as stymied by their own antagonisms as by the opposition of the French regime. When the First Muslim Congress in June 1936, failed to invite Messali, his followers created disorders for the executive meeting of the Congress the following January. Despite his support for the regeneration of Islam in Algeria, Messali was suspect in the eyes of the Ulama for his class rhetoric and affiliations. The Ulama seemed to move more easily with the men of the Federation—despite the latter's secularist bent (like that of Kemal Ataturk or Habib ben Ali Bourguiba) and sympathies for the French. The PCA, for its part, had defined Messali as its chief opponent in the late thirties, and so sought allies among the other two factions of Muslim opinion. The general trend toward nationalism around the time of World War II resulted for a time in a united front (without the Communists or Bendjelloul) behind Abbas in 1944. But within a year the movement fell apart as the Messalists came more and more to impose their view on the alliance. Again, after

11. Sivan, *Communisme et nationalisme en Algérie.*

the election frauds of June 1951, there was a short-lived Algerian Front for the Defense and Respect of Freedom. But when the revolution finally broke on November 1, 1954, the initiative came not from the coordinated union of these various groups but from a splinter organization of Messali's MTLD.[12]

Perhaps the French believed that their mixture of firmness and liberality in handling Muslim grievances was what held the Muslim factions apart. The conversion of Abbas to nationalism during World War II, and the publication of the Manifesto in 1943, prompted Charles de Gaulle, then in Algiers, the provisional capital of France, to make a speech (December 12, 1943) promising increased social and political equality for the Muslim population. The product of his Declaration, the Ordinance of March 7, 1944, went even further than the prewar Blum-Viollette proposal by allowing certain categories of Muslims—estimated at 60,000— to become French citizens without the abandonment of their Quranic status. The way was now open, in principle at least, for the gradual enlargement of this group and the eventual assimilation thereby of the Muslim community to France, although the Ordinance did enshrine the notion of two equal electoral colleges, one for the Europeans and a handful of Muslims, the other for the bulk of the indigenous population. Subsequently, the Law of August 17, 1945, took yet another unprecedented step by assuring universal male suffrage for the Muslim community and by giving the second college the right to elect a number of deputies to the Constituent Assembly equal to the number selected by the first college. However short these measures may have fallen by the highest democratic standards, they nonetheless represented tremendous innovations in the style of French government in Algeria.

The Law of August 17, 1945, was all the more forceful since it followed the outbreak of the most serious threat to French sovereignty in Algeria since the Mokrani insurrection of 1871. On May 8, 1945, amidst the celebrations throughout Algeria over the

12. For a general account, see Charles André Julien, *L'Afrique du Nord en marche* (Julliard, Paris, 1952); Claude Martin, *Histoire de l'Algérie française, 1830–1962* (Editions des Quatre Fils Aymon, Paris, 1963), Part III, Chapter 5; Roger Le Tourneau, *Evolution politique de l'Afrique du Nord musulmane, 1920–1961* (Armand Colin, Paris, 1962).

defeat of Germany, Muslim riots broke out in the department of Constantine, most notably in the towns of Sétif and Guelma. The following day, bands of Muslims roamed the countryside striking at isolated European farms and hamlets. In all, over 100 Europeans, many of them local political or administrative officials, were killed. The aspect of the French response which calls for the most comment was its unbridled fierceness, most closely linked in all probability to the firm conviction that any sign of hesitation or show of mercy would be interpreted as weakness and so encourage the rebellion to spread. The racism of hastily formed vigilante groups and the fears of undermanned military units doubtless contributed to the harsh French reaction.[13] But the common denominator to most opinion in European circles from the left to the right, in metropolitan France as in Algeria, was that France authority must not be found hesitant or wanting.[14] The same attitude had been evident, of course, on many occasions in earlier times, but its spontaneous regeneration in 1945 had causes, as we shall see, more directly related to the contemporary period. Indeed, this conviction was to be one of the most reiterated themes of French political opinion in regard to the revolution: liberality should extend only so far as it enhanced the French presence; and any hesitation was a sign of weakness sure to feed disorder.

Well before the incidents of May 1945, however, Muslim nationalists—with the exception of Bendjelloul and the PCA—had reacted negatively to the French proposals for assimilation contained in the Ordinance of March 7, 1944. Abbas had created the Association des Amis du Manifeste et de la Liberté (AML), which had obtained the backing of the Ulama and the clandestine PPA, in order to organize protests against this policy and to marshall support for an independent Algeria. When, fourteen months later, the Sétif rebellion was to occur, Interior Minister Adrien Tixier would hold these groups responsible for the tragedy, claiming that they had incited the local population to riot. Sub-

13. The number of Muslims killed is variously estimated at from six to forty-five thousand. In addition to local vigilantes and ground forces, a French cruiser bombarded some coastal villages and French aviation struck forty-four hamlets.
14. See, for example, the comments collected in Robert Aron, *Les Origines de la Guerre d'Algérie*, Chapter 2.

sequently, the AML was dissolved by government order, and Abbas and Messali were placed under arrest.

Neither leader could therefore participate in the elections to the First Constituent Assembly held in October 1945. For the Muslim college with thirteen seats, the result was an assimilationist sweep, the Communists capturing two seats, the Socialists four, and Bendjelloul's Federation the remaining seven. Abbas was released the following spring, however, just in time to set up a new movement, the Union Démocratique du Manifeste Algérien (UDMA), for the June elections to the Second Constituent. Bendjelloul's proposals that France increase the assimilation of Algeria having been turned a deaf ear by the First Constituent Assembly, Abbas's program calling for the effective independence of Algeria rallied broad nationalist support. Despite his apparent mandate from the Muslim population—Abbas's group won 71 percent of the vote and eleven of the thirteen seats—the Second Constituent Assembly paid little heed to his appeals.

As a result, the UDMA refused to compete in the elections to the first legislature of the Fourth Republic, held in November 1946. Attention then centered on Messali, who had been recently liberated from prison and had founded yet another political group, the Mouvement pour le Triomphe des Libertés Démocratiques (MTLD). In these November elections, the MTLD gained five of the fifteen seats, but its vote might have been larger had there been a larger turnout and had the party not been banned from running in the department of Oran and one of the three electoral districts of Constantine.[15] The UDMA made its showing in the indirect election to the Council of the Republic where, despite the interior minister's opposition, it gained four of the seven seats.

It may be recalled that the Second Constituent Assembly had decided that one of the first responsibilities of the new legislature would be to define the exact political status of Algeria. While the new Constitution provided for a French Union to give a new structure to the empire as a whole, individual territories were to negotiate bilateral agreements to guide their relationships with Paris. True to the tradition of French legislation for Algeria,

---

15. *Notes et Etudes Documentaires*, number 678.

however, the solution ultimately devised in the summer of 1947 satisfied neither of the principal parties involved: the entire Muslim delegation abstained from the vote on the Statute of Algeria while nine of the fifteen Europeans voted against it with two abstentions. To the Europeans, the Statute's provisions for a local Algerian Assembly seemed to pave the way for eventual independence by providing a platform to serve nationalist agitation. To the Muslims, on the other hand, the Statute was flawed both in its form (since it did not provide even in the distant future for the existence of an Algerian state), and in its content, since the Assembly it created had only the most meager of powers—and even these were effectively under the control of the European minority.

Limited as the Statute's substantive measures for change were, however, they were never to be enjoyed. Only two months after passage of the Statute, the municipal elections of October 1947 signaled the polarization of the two communities in Algeria. Among the Europeans, the non-Marxist parties had strengthened their organization and increased their following, while among the Muslims, Messali's MTLD made a strong showing, emerging as the leading nationalist force in the country. As a result, the settlers moved into action. At the instigation of René Mayer, minister of finance and deputy from Constantine, the liberal Governor General Yves Chatigneau was dismissed and the law-and-order Minister of Education Marcel-Edmon Naegelen, a Socialist, was put in his place.

Messali made use of his victory in the October elections to prepare his campaign for the first Algerian Assembly, scheduled to be selected in January 1948, then delayed until April. During this time, the French administration and the settler community developed what Charles André Julien has aptly called a veritable "war psychosis."[16] Evidence was adduced demonstrating the great organizational powers of the MTLD, its preparation of a clandestine army of national liberation, its use of threats against Muslims who disputed its monopoly of power over the electors to the second college. Messali's alleged warning to the Europeans— "the suitcase or the coffin"—was everywhere repeated.

16. Julien, *L'Afrique du Nord en marche,* p. 324.

Convinced that if the elections were held fairly, Messali would win the great majority of the ballots cast by a credulous and intimidated second college, the administration set what was to become a precedent in Algeria: it reported fraudulent election returns. Of the sixty seats in the college, "independents" (French appointees, that is) won forty-one, Independent Socialists two, the MTLD nine, and the UDMA eight. In the first college, on the other hand, where election results are considered accurate, the Europeans ratified the action of the administration by voting only four Socialists and one Communist to their sixty-man section of the Assembly. The other fifty-five seats went to a center-right coalition pledged to the defense of French Algeria.

Though Naegelen's successors were able to reproduce the fraudulent election practices, his unequalled flights of rhetoric in the midst of all this could not be matched. The day following the first tricked election—soon to be called "good joke" (*bonne blague*) elections—Naegelen congratulated the people of Algeria on the "calm and dignity" with which they had fulfilled their Republican duty. Some weeks later he declared:

We assure liberty to those who deserve it, but there can be liberty only when the liberty of others is respected. Those who would threaten this country with danger, even with terror, those who would use violence to impose their will, let them have no illusions! . . . We will crush terror, we will prevent violence, we will make certain order and justice reign in this land.[17]

And again:

The intentions of France are clear. She wishes that henceforth in Algeria there be only citizens mixed in the equality of their rights and their obligations. . . . Of eight million Algerians we would make eight million equal men and seal their union such that it can never be put into question. And when we speak thus, we are not motivated by thoughts of national or imperial domination but by the obviousness of reason and simple human concern.[18]

Having rigged the elections, Naegelen saw to it that the administrative reforms specified by the Statute—suppression of the *communes mixtes*, freedom of the Muslim cult, teaching of Arabic in

17. *Notes et Etudes Documentaires,* number 919.
18. *Journal officiel* of the Algerian Assembly, May 21, 1948, p. 25.

the schools—remained dead letter.[19] All in all, he congratulated himself on his "very firm policy in regard to agitators and the violent" which, he claimed, had inspired "a return of confidence" within the Muslim community.[20]

Paris accepted these practices so easily, in part because the government had learned the virtues of firmness in facing down the serious Communist strikes of the preceding November. This had been the time of the "Great Fear," when a form of "collective psychosis," according to Georgette Elgey, had gripped France as the first giant wave of the Cold War broke upon the land.[21] Jules Moch, the Socialist interior minister who had successfully dealt with the Communists during this trial of strength, was also the minister responsible for Algeria. He was therefore charged to receive before the National Assembly the Communist-sponsored motion to annul the rigged April 1948 elections to the Algerian Assembly. Moch was careful to say that he had no sure evidence that the elections in Algeria had indeed been tricked. But he insisted at some length on the unworthiness of the MTLD to compete in a democratic manner. He cited instances of Messalist intimidation, of MTLD's seditious sloganeering, of its alleged links with the old Moroccan revolutionary Abd el-Krim (then in Cairo), and of its plans to falsify the electoral returns. "We must watch out not to reason as though we were at home about a country where, unfortunately, political education is still rudimentary," Moch warned. And he repeated approvingly some of Naegelen's statements concerning the need for authority first of all to be firm in Algeria. He concluded: "I am sure, ladies and gentlemen, that there is not a Republican in the Assembly who would not make the words of Governor General Naegelen his own. In any case, this is the policy of the government to which he has given an eloquent formulation. (Applause from the left, center, and right.)" The Assembly then voted to table the Communist motion for a debate on the Algerian elections.[22]

19. Articles 53, 56, and 57 of the Algerian Statute, the application thereof "to be the object of decisions of the Algerian Assembly."
20. Undated speech reprinted in "Situation et évolution politique de l'Algérie en 1948 et 1949," published by the Service d'Information du Cabinet du Gouverneur Général de l'Algérie.
21. Elgey, *La République des illusions,* Part 2, Chapter 2.
22. *Journal officiel,* May 4, 1948, pp. 2490–2491.

The debate over how liberal to be toward Algeria had thus quickly become academic as the contradiction between French liberality and continued French sovereignty opened with the first elections to the Algerian Assembly, scarcely nine months after the Statute of Algeria had been voted. Here a Socialist governor general and a Socialist minister of the interior collaborated, first to fix the elections, then to prevent their annulment by the National Assembly. The Communist deputies alone protested as a group. Defeated by the maneuvers of Moch in the Assembly, they took their case before the Commission of the Interior within the National Assembly, and to the Council of the Republic. In each instance, they were refused a decision and were referred to the Council of State, an administrative body which refused to hear their petition. In the Assembly of the French Union, however, the party was more successful. On June 18, 1948, with Communists and Socialists together, this Assembly voted to send an investigating team to Algeria to inquire into the irregularities in the vote. For just an instant life seemed to stir in this already moribund institution. Then the prime minister notified the Assembly that such matters were outside its competence.[23]

Thereafter, in local, Algerian, and national elections, the French systematically altered the returns for the second college. Naegelen was removed from office in 1951, after an unseemly public row with an official who refused to follow this procedure, but his successor, Roger Léonard, former chief of police of Paris appointed by Moch, continued the tradition.[24] In the 1951 and 1954 elections to the Algerian Assembly (half of whose seats were renewed every three years), the UDMA and the MTLD found the few places they held taken from them, just as the June 1951 elections to the second legislature in Paris saw them eliminated from the National Assembly and the Council of the Republic.

After the 1951 elections, the Communists tried once again (albeit more lukewarmly) to have the Algerian returns annulled by proposing that a committee investigate evidence on the vote in

23. Ivo Rens, *L'Assemblée algérienne* (Editions A. Pedone, Paris, 1957), pp. 101–106. *Journal officiel* of the Assembly of the French Union, June 18, 1948.

24. Naegelen subsequently denied that he rigged the elections, going so far as to insist that he took measures to see this would not happen. See his *Mission en Algérie* (Flammarion, Paris, 1962), pp. 64–66.

North Africa. This time the French National Assembly was obliged to take a stand, since it alone could validate these returns. In retrospect, the event appears momentous: it was the last occasion on which the French conscience could act to insure that liberal democratic principles were followed in Algeria, whatever the cost in other terms. On August 9, 1951, however, by a vote of 316 to 55 (including 41 Communists) the deputies to the National Assembly turned down the motion and so sanctioned explicitly not only a practice contrary to democratic principles, but also a pathetically ineffective manner of dealing with popular grievances in Algeria. It should be noted that Socialists Guy Mollet, Christian Pineau, Edouard Depreux, and Jules Moch voted with the majority.[25] With this vote a gradual evolution in French rhetoric may be said to have come to an end. Previously, many Frenchmen had maintained that liberality and sovereignty would complement each other in a mutually reinforcing fashion. Now the argument shifted ground. Henceforth, it was to be a question of means and ends; French sovereignty would be the instrument to bring about the eventually promised end of liberty. It was only a question of time before this hypocrisy would lead France from a policy of fraud to one of force in Algeria.

Meanwhile, political affairs in the first college took an unexpected turn late in 1950. The change was not due to the action either of the Socialists, whose base had fallen sharply since 1945, or of the Communists, who after an initial decline from the number of votes received for the First Constituent Assembly had just managed to hold their own.[26] Instead, the intransigence of the European community was for a brief while checked by the about-face of Jacques Chevallier, deputy to the National Assembly from Algiers. A man of hitherto impeccably reactionary credentials, Chevallier wrote in a series of articles in *Echo d'Alger* of December 1950 that the old attitudes characteristic of the French were mistaken and that a new climate of reconciliation between the two communities of Algeria was essential. Thereupon, Chevallier resigned his post in Paris to be elected to the Algerian

25. *Journal officiel*, August 9, 1951; the breakdown of the vote is given under August 10, pp. 6284ff and 6332–6333.

26. Election returns are reported for Algeria in *Le Monde*, October 24, 1945; June 4, 1946; and June 20, 1951.

Assembly in February 1951, there to form a bloc of Intergroup Liberals dedicated to this end. The group's heterogeneity and the vagueness of its program having apparently undercut the spirit of renovation, Chevallier resigned the Assembly to become mayor of Algiers in the elections of April–May 1953. Preferring to work with "quasi-rebels rather than servants," Chevallier saw to the free election of the municipality's second college and found his city council composed of thirty-six Europeans and twenty-five members of the MTLD.

The most remarkable thing about Chevallier's experience was its uniqueness. Elsewhere in Algeria electoral fraud and political repression continued unabated. Worse still, the social and administrative reforms which might conceivably have prepared the ground for political liberalization were neglected. The achievements of the Chatigneau administration slowly disintegrated.[27] On the other hand, it is important not to exaggerate Chevallier's attempt as the promise of a new day. As late as 1958, when he published what might be called a memoir of his political life in Algeria, Chevallier was still thinking in terms of reforms little more progressive than those of the Statute of 1947. Like so many others, Chevallier was a reformist; it was never his intention to prepare the way for the end of French sovereignty over Algeria.[28]

Nevertheless, to stress only the repressive features of French sovereignty in Algeria—what Naegelen, speaking of his own responsibilities, once called his "smiling and benevolent authority" —is to miss the key to its role in the outbreak of the revolution. For it was the contradiction between a partial and sporadic liberalism allowing opposition to form, and the subsequent neglect or repression then meted out which spelled danger. Nothing is more disastrous to a relatively weak government than for it to let a powerful opposition form only to refuse to honor its demands. Yet, as we have seen, in the quarter century preceding the revolution, it is precisely this that occurred. The French permitted the organization of the PCA, the reformist Ulama, the Federation, and, more haltingly, the Messalists before World War II. Following the war, a Muslim labor union formed, democratic

27. Julien, *L'Afrique du Nord en marche*, p. 335.
28. Jacques Chevallier, *Nous, Algériens* (Calmann-Lévy, Paris, 1958).

pledges were made, some free elections were held, and even when the balloting was rigged, a pretense of democracy was usually maintained by allowing political campaigns. Moreover, French administration outside the *communes de plein exercice,* never terribly efficient for want of funds, suffered greatly during the war and continued to decline thereafter. This greatly facilitated the work of the rebels who chose as the first center of action the Aurès, a mountainous region ineffectively governed by the French authoritie's.[29] In retrospect, then, the connivances of the French in Algeria with their political machinations seem as much pathetic as outrageous. Certainly, restrictions and repression were a prominent feature of French rule there. The administration placed informers; it censored literature and public meetings, harassed political activities, partially disenfranchised the Muslim population, tortured suspected subversives (in 1950, for example, as the result of an alleged MTLD plot), and discriminated in all manner of way economically and socially. Yet France had been liberal enough in spirit, and Paris forceful enough on occasion, to guarantee that certain freedoms were at least intermittently permitted. In short, the political climate *did* permit critical voices to be raised, opposition leadership to emerge, and organizations hostile to the French presence to begin operations years before the revolution commenced.

Settler as well as Muslim extremism was profoundly affected by these contradictions. When the chips were down—when either the settlers decided to be intransigent or the natives looked particularly threatening—the settlers could count on support from Paris. At other times, however, they were obliged to maintain their guard, convinced, as François Quilici, one of the leading "ultra" spokesmen put it, that "years of softness, of weakness, and especially of ideological dreaming" had led to a "weakness steeped with scruples" that any day might undermine the French order in Algeria.[30] Nor was General Aumeran, another settler spokesman, being blind when he lambasted the "untimely in-

29. See the complaints of Jacques Soustelle in this regard, *Aimée et souffrante Algérie* (Plon, Paris, 1956), pp. 25–26; Guy Mollet, *Journal officiel,* March 27, 1957, p. 11; and Georges Chaffard, *Les Carnets sécrets de la décolonization* (Calmann-Lévy, Paris, 1967), II, 14ff.

30. *Journal officiel,* November 12, 1954, p. 4949.

trusion of neophyte metropolitan reformers whose interference always results in a deplorable division of hearts and minds."[31]

There was, after all, sound logic to the proposition that genuine political reform would only pave the way to the end of French sovereignty over Algeria. The delusion of well-intentioned liberals had always been to pretend the contrary: reform sincerely applied, so they imagined, would finally cement the marriage of Algeria to France. Had reforms been long-ranged and sure, had they confronted the serious economic and political problems of the country, and had they been started early enough to rally some Muslim support and to prepare the ground for more, then liberality might have created the conditions for the integration of France and Algeria. Otherwise, as Aumeran had put it, the efforts of these "neophyte metropolitan reformers" only unsettled the system. The words of the first governor general of Algeria under the Third Republic in 1871 were surely as true seventy-five years later: "If in one stroke we created two million citizens, the French minority would be politically suffocated. What would then happen to the base of our domination?"[32] Given the accumulated host of social and economic grievances of the Muslim community, its heavy numerical preponderance, the international climate, and the expressed mood of its leaders, the settlers—not the liberals—had for the moment the better argument by far: France could not be both democratic and sovereign in Algeria after 1945. Caught between their scruples and their ambitions, the French tried to effect a compromise by way of reforms—simply to discover that all the good intentions finding their way into legislation and culminating in the Statute of Algeria of 1947 aroused only the enmity of the chief parties concerned.

For to the Muslim population as well as to the settlers, French policy was exasperating. The clear failure of assimilationist or liberal federationist dreams became apparent with the shelving of the Blum-Viollette proposals and the sabotage of all the progressive features of the Statute of Algeria of 1947, beginning in 1948. For a time, the only other alternative, violence, seemed equally unacceptable, since the harshness of the French repression of the

31. *Journal officiel,* February 2, 1955, p. 604.
32. Governor General Gueydon, cited in Ageron, *Les Algériens musulmans,* p. 346n.

riots of May 1945, had made prudent men of many of the radical nationalists. But it was a faction within the Messalist movement, grouped for the most part around its clandestine paramilitary arm, the Special Organization (OS) which, under the inspiration of nationalists based primarily in Cairo and working with the support of Gamal Abdel Nasser, eventually sparked the revolution.[33]

Once the revolution began, the French liberals continued to talk reform, making up now in stridence for what their program still lacked in substance. No longer, however, could the contradiction between democracy and sovereignty be papered over with legalistic formulas meaning nothing in practice. Forced to choose, the French opted for sovereignty, with reformism becoming a mask donned by the liberals as they moved to join the forces of repression. Talk now as they would continue to do of reform, in practice they used force. Yet what was possible in 1947 —and here, too, of course, the options were narrowly restricted and had at least to provide for meaningful Home Rule for Algeria —was certainly no longer possible in 1957. As Chapter 1 attempted to demonstrate in discussing the framework law of that year, the majority of French deputies in 1957 proved insensitive to a decade's developments, acting for all the world in the last year of the Fourth Republic's life as though some formula short of the Statute of 1947 might yet save French sovereignty in Algeria. Self-deception had become the Republic's trademark.

33. William Quandt, *Revolution and Political Leadership: Algeria, 1954–1958* (M.I.T. Press, Cambridge, 1969).

6 The Enforcement of the Consensus on Algeria

Sometime after the turn of the century, as we have seen, it became apparent that under colonialism Algeria would never become economically and socially secure. During the interwar years, the consequences of this failure acquired form in the political organization of various sectors of the Muslim community, and in the increasingly bitter expression by the community of a variety of grievances against the character of French rule. The shelving of the Blum-Viollette proposals in 1938, the sabotage of the Statute of 1947, and the decision not to honor the pledge to let the Muslim population be democratically represented in the National Assembly, confirmed French rule as reactionary and set the stage in political terms for a violent reaction. Deprived by their own hand of political leverage within the Muslim community, the French were unable to stem or satisfactorily to detour a jacquerie which, in the style unique to our century, had organized leadership and direction. For by an irony of history, the barriers which the French had set up to keep the Muslims from entry into the European city turned out in time to be a defense behind which the rebellion could rally. French sabotage of elections beginning in 1948, and their appointment of Muslims of unquestioned loyalty (the so-called *beni-oui-ouis* or Uncle Toms) to political posts thereafter made it virtually impossible to establish a credible native elite to counter the FLN once the revolution was underway. For now, whoever agreed to work with the French was hard put to avoid the taint of sell-out and corruption. Economic and social exclusion had created a vast impoverished Muslim mass available for revolutionary mobilization, while political decisions had cut the links between the French and virtually all the organized elites of the Muslim community. French efforts to right this error, to root a moderate "third force" political structure within the Algerian people so as to create the hoped for *interlocuteur valable* with whom they could negotiate a settlement with more favorable conditions than those demanded by the FLN, were to prove one of the most frustrating aspects of the revolutionary period for them.

Such a reconstruction of the policy toward Algeria before November 1954, however, gives only a slight indication of what the French response would be to an insurrection once it was underway.[1] With the exception of the massive, indiscriminate retaliation to rioting in the Constantinois in May 1945, Paris counted more on fraud, negligence, and pious hopes for the future than on force to maintain control over the three North African departments. Willing Algeria to be at once democratic and French—contradictory policies whose incompatibility could only momentarily be ignored—Paris had begun to fantasize the political silence in Algeria as tranquillity. Everyone knew that from the spring of 1948 all the Algerian elections were rigged. Nonetheless, Vincent Auriol, president of the Republic and a Socialist, apparently astonished no one when he returned from a trip through Algeria to report "unforgetable signs of affection, loyalty, and confidence." Everywhere "the people cried their love for France."[2] In the same manner, many would profess surprise when the rebellion later broke out, maintaining that after "nine years of calm" (dating from the Sétif uprising in 1945) such agitation was not to be expected.

How, then, do we explain the determined move from fraud to force when the uprising demonstrated its seriousness? To do this, we must turn from Algeria to France, and ask not what France

---

1. For the conduct of the revolution, see among others, Alf Andrew Heggoy, *Insurgency and Counter-Insurgency in Algeria* (University of Indiana, Bloomington, 1972); Arslan Humbaraci, *Algeria, A Revolution that Failed* (Pall Mall Press, London, 1966); Quandt, *Revolution and Political Leadership*.

2. *Combat*, June 7, 1949.

meant to Algeria but what Algeria meant to France. Chapter 7 will review the variety of interests—moral, economic, political, and strategic—which together made up the French stake in Algeria. But, to repeat a point made in the Introduction and Chapter 1 of this book, the major stake the French had in Algeria was a certain image of themselves in the world on the basis of which they had come to a colonial consensus whose terms dictated the preservation of their sovereignty in North Africa. Analysts of the difficulty of French decolonization typically fail to pose the issue in these terms, assuming instead that it was resolve on these matters which precisely was lacking. Most commonly held at fault for the inability of the Fourth Republic to accommodate itself to postwar realities was the French political system, whose short-comings made adaptation to the urgent and delicate problems of a greatly changed world virtually impossible. The weakness of the system, so this general argument runs, permitted the concentration of forces dedicated to the preservation of the empire and their eventual veto power over the acts of the Republic. A colonial consensus? Once again students of French affairs look wistfully to the British, for in Paris no such thing was possible, and, in default of the Fourth Republic, one was articulated by the military in league with the settlers and various right-wing opportunists in France. Not a colonial consensus, but "indecision," "immobilism," and "division," or so we are told, characterized the political order and so were responsible for the vicissitudes of decolonization.

Yet, time and again, beneath the invective of political division, one finds a shared anguish in France at the passing of national greatness, a shared humiliation at a century of defeats, a shared belief that France should retain her independence in a hostile world, a shared fear that her inability to regain national rank would be the consequence of her own internal decadence (a favorite word of the period)—all brought to rest on the determination that the colonies, but particularly Algeria, remain French. Studies that obscure this common commitment foster a sort of collective amnesia that has seemed to set in since de Gaulle's announcement of Algerian independence. Better to heap abuse on the system than to remember the passions, the hypocrisy, the games of self-deception that were the common currency of the time and whose contribution to the political and moral defeat of the Republic were fundamental. Ironically, such studies repeat in their fashion the essential mistake in perception made by the leaders of the Fourth Republic, who held that France was being defeated in Algeria not by the historical anachronism of her goals there but by the spectacle of her parliamentary weakness and the reaction this produced in the Muslim population. Division, immobilism, and indecision were characteristic of the National Assembly only at the point where it began to become obvious that repression was failing. As investigations of such key governments as those of Socialists Ramadier and Mollet illustrate, a colonial consensus amounting to a policy of maintaining French sovereignty with minor concessions to local nationalist leaders launched the disastrous careers of France, first in Indochina, later in Algeria. Socialists were not, it should be reiterated, the most adamant proponents of the colonial consensus, but their presence clearly behind its banner demonstrates the extent to which the mind of the French political elite was in agreement.

After the fall of the Ramadier government in November 1947 (a government whose contribution to the involvement in Indochina and to defining the terms of the connection between Algeria and France has already been reviewed), Socialists continued to hold cabinet posts, but none was prime minister until the electoral victory of the Republican Front in December 1955 and the investiture of Guy Mollet the following month. Mollet's credentials showed him to be a man of the left within the party. At the 38th Congress of the SFIO in 1946, Mollet had presented a motion reproaching "revisionism" among the party leaders (Blum, Mayer, Ramadier, etc.) and recalling the movement to its allegiance to the truths of Marxism, especially to the reality of the class struggle. Mollet's motion passed, and for the first time in the history of the party, the *rapport moral* prepared by the leadership went down to defeat. The following year, Mollet acted to take over the party organization. But the move coincided with the official inauguration of the Cold War, which in France found expression in a serious wave of Communist-led strikes on the one hand, and in the strong showing of de Gaulle's newly formed party, the RPF, at the municipal elections of October on the other.[3]

The result was an alliance of the Socialists with the parties of the center-right against the twin threats of Gaullism and Communism. Future events only confirmed this orientation as both the party and the French nation gradually moved to the right politically. Over the years, the class and geographic support of the Socialists had changed so that the party was less urban and working class and increasingly representative of white-collar workers and the lower middle class outside the larger cities. At the same time, the altering configuration of party relationships cast the Socialists into the position the Radicals once had enjoyed. "Comfortably installed in national and local administration, and strategically placed at the political center of gravity," writes Philip Williams, "SFIO grew increasingly reluctant to disturb the workings of the system."[4] So Maurice Duverger, a leading writer on the party at this time, describes it in the early fifties:

It is precisely the case that the SFIO has become "embourgeoisé," that it is becoming increasingly conservative, that certain of its leaders are corrupt or incapable (or both), that it no longer has a doctrine or a program, that its influence is in decline, that it can no longer renew its membership, and that young voters are turning away from it.[5]

Even so, the party stood at the left wing of the colonial consensus. It did not share the military's optimism about Indochina, nor the fierce determination of the MRP to win there, and it began calling for negotiations with Ho Chi Minh years before the Geneva settlement. But as we have seen, SFIO allegiance to the colonial consensus was something more than forced upon it by the impossibility of working with the Communists. Before the

---

3. Bruce Graham, *The French Socialists and Tripartisme, 1944–1947* (Weidenfeld and Nicolson, London, 1965); Daniel Ligou, *Histoire du socialisme en France, 1871–1961* (Presses Universitaires de France, Paris, 1962), pp. 543–545.

4. Philip Williams, *Crisis and Compromise*, p. 105.

5. Maurice Duverger, "SFIO: mort ou transfiguration?" *Les Temps Modernes*, numbers 112–113, p. 1863. For later figures on class and geographic support of the SFIO at this time, see Maurice Duverger, ed., *Partis politiques et classes sociales en France* (Cahiers de la Fondation Nationale des Science Politiques, Paris, n.d.), pp. 195–209.

end of Communist participation in government in May 1947, the
Socialists had shown themselves to the right of the PCF with
regard to the Congress of Black Africans called by the Rassemblement Démocratique Africain (RDA) in October 1946, the
war effort in Indochina beginning in November 1946, the drafts
for the Statute of Algeria drawn up in the winter of 1946 to 1947,
and the repression of the nationalist uprising in Madagascar in
March and April 1947.

Just as the Socialist governments of Blum and Ramadier were
key participants in crucial decisions made in regard to Indochina
in 1946 and 1947, so the Mollet government, which assumed
office in January 1956, took the decisive steps that assured the
protracted character of the Algerian conflict. When Mollet left
office in May 1957 after the longest term as prime minister in the
history of the Fourth Republic, he had irrevocably set the direction of the regime on a disaster course. This was not the result of
the "system" working its haphazard way and finally reaching the
point of no return when the forces of anger and frustration which
had acquired organization strength issued an ultimatum in May
1958, thus ending the life of the regime. Rather, closer analysis
reveals this to have been the result of a calculated policy that
simply refused to accept the possibility of Algerian independence. Not indecision but decision marked this determining
period of the conflict.

The initial point to emphasize is the new mood of confidence
following the electoral victory of the Republican Front early in
1956. Ever since Mendès-France had taken matters in hand and
ended the terrible Indochinese War in the summer of 1954,
France had seemed to acquire a new ability to resolve the colonial
problems plaguing her. After Geneva, Mendès-France had gone
on to end the confrontation in Tunisia where, since the spring of
1954, some 70,000 French troops had been held down by guerrilla action. Here Mendès-France offered Bourguiba full "internal autonomy" for Tunisia under the concept of "independence
within interdependence." However vague this formula, Bourguiba had accepted it and was able the following year, despite
powerful opposition within Tunisia by those who distrusted the
French and were backed by Cairo, to conclude an important
agreement with Edgar Faure's government, which in the interim

had come to power. This government maintained a strong record of realistic adjustments to nationalist demands from the overseas possessions. In addition to completing successfully Mendès-France's work in Tunisia (as well as with the Fezzan which was returned to Libya, and the Indian enclaves which were returned to New Delhi), Faure began to prepare for the independence of Togo now that the British intention to withdraw from its African mandates was established. But Faure's most outstanding achievement in colonial affairs was to end peacefully the Moroccan crisis which had festered since the French had deposed the Sultan in the summer of 1953.[6]

In regard to Algeria, however, the Faure government had been less innovative. Then, on August 20, 1955, an uprising in the Algerian town of Philippeville finally brought home to French public opinion the seriousness of the struggle there. Mollet and Mendès-France, joined together on a common platform of the Republican Front, were determined to make Algeria the primary issue of their campaign and to base their appeal on a pledge to end what Mollet then called "this moronic war without end."[7]

Indeed the Socialists had already begun preparing for this approach in the months preceding the electoral campaign. Force without reform could not work, they explained, and the Faure government in their eyes lacked the ability to undertake the difficult task of bringing about the changes Algeria so badly needed. Thus, in March 1955, during the debate over the government's request for emergency powers in Algeria; Socialist spokesman François Vals explained his party's refusal to vote the request, its refusal to subscribe to a policy of force: "The source of the disorder is misery, unemployment, the Statute of Algeria that was never applied, and the reforms always promised but never implemented. Social, economic, and political measures that look to dry up the trouble will be much more effective in re-establishing order than the state of emergency asked for by the government."[8] Again in October, the party refused to vote

6. One of the most readable general accounts in English for developments in North Africa is Charles Gallagher, *The United States and North Africa* (Harvard University Press, Cambridge, 1963).

7. Mollet in *L'Express*, reprinted in *Le Populaire*, December 20, 1955.

8. *Journal officiel*, March 30, 1955, p. 2136.

confidence in the Faure government, saying it lacked the ability to draw up and execute the reforms necessary in Algeria.[9]

When the electoral campaign opened in December 1955, the Socialists tried to recreate something of the mood of the Popular Front. Headlines in the party paper, *Le Populaire,* denounced the forces of reaction and stressed the readiness of the Republican Front to take on the problems confronting the nation. In colonial matters, to which the coalition of the moment gave primary attention, this energetic mood was particularly evident. On December 20, *Le Populaire* reprinted a lead article by Mollet that had recently appeared in *L'Express* where the Socialist leader most notably denounced right-wing settler groups and colonial administrative staffs which, as experience in Morocco, Tunisia, and Indochina had demonstrated, tried to undermine liberal policies formulated in Paris. Mollet called for cashiering these groups and dealing instead with qualified leaders of the colonial peoples rather than with figureheads without popular backing (such as Bao Dai had been in Indochina, and Bin Arafa in Morocco).

The first duty of the government that will be formed after the election will be to restore peace in North Africa. What we must do before all else is to stop lying, to stop repeating the same errors of Indochina, Morocco, and Tunisia. Of course we must protect the Algerian populations, but we must stop this blind and imbecilic repression.

A speech by Mendès-France at Marseilles on December 26, and a televised address by Mollet four days later closed the Republican Front's campaign. Militarily, protection of civilians would continue, but not on the scale of "blind repression, unworthy of France." Economically, Mollet promised "massive agricultural and industrial investments, land distribution, and the distribution of goods of primary necessity. This will be worth more than troop reinforcements and police." Politically, their program was the most vague, but they planned for the Algerian Assembly to be dissolved and free elections to be held within a period of six months in order to provide the people of Algeria a voice in their future.[10] The Republican Front's victory on January 2, 1956,

9. See statements by Alain Savary and Edouard Depreux, *Journal officiel,* October 13, 1955, pp. 5101, 5104–5105; and October 18, p. 5145.
10. *L'Express,* December 27, 1955; *Le Populaire,* January 2, 1956.

demonstrated the confidence of the French people that this program would end the struggle in Algeria. For the first time since 1945, the Socialist electoral vote registered an increase. Mollet and Mendès-France would take control of the Algerian situation before the conflict was too advanced and so spare the Republic a re-enactment of the long ordeal of Indochina.

Nothing better illustrates the course Mollet's government was soon to take than the figures on French troop levels in Algeria. With under 200,000 men in the area when he took office in late January, Mollet decided to call up the reserves and commit the conscript army to the struggle. Before the end of the year, some 500,000 French soldiers were engaged in the "pacification" of Algeria. "The action for Algeria will be effective only with the confident support of the entire nation, with its total commitment," Guy Mollet put it in taking these measures.[11] Thus, within a matter of months, France found herself wholeheartedly involved in quelling the revolt by bringing about a substantial escalation of the conflict there.

The basic ingredient in Mollet's program was one with an established pedigree in Fourth Republic France: generosity backed by strength could bring the rebellion to an end. At no point did Mollet contemplate independence for Algeria. What he did propose was a sketch for a new political statute for the country, a primary feature of which was the Balkanization of Algeria into a number of territorial units weakly federated in Algiers. Under the Bourgès-Maunoury and the Gaillard governments that followed Mollet, this idea got caught up into the new framework law for Algeria that was finally adopted in February 1958 (see Chapter 1). Mollet's shortcoming, in other words, was his inability to plan for any developments other than reform in Algeria, to fail to see the contradiction between liberalism and French sovereignty there.

But the principal criticism directed against Mollet both at that time and later was that he *abandoned* reformism. Thus, most commentators date what they consider his fatal move by his visit to Algiers one week after his investiture. Mendès-France had called for such a gesture from the new prime minister during the

11. *Le Populaire*, April 16, 1956.

election campaign, and Mollet decided to make it. There on February 6, 1956, however, an unexpected welcome of rotten eggs and tomatoes from the European population resulted in an important modification of Mollet's Algerian policy. Previously he had apparently accepted the anticolonialist line, considering only the wealthy *colons* as committed partisans of French Algeria. Now he saw the strength of this passion among "the little whites" toward whom he and his party were traditionally sympathetic. Rallying to the side of these people, Mollet appeased them:

You have been depicted as colonialists. I do not share this view. . . . These farmers, these employees, these tradespeople, these teachers, these doctors, these men who have been established in Algeria for several generations and have their families, their homes, and their dead here—since my arrival I have heard the voice of all of them and I have been greatly moved by it. . . . These men—you who are listening—believed that France was going to abandon them. I have understood their despair, the profound despair that holds their whole being in its grip. This is why I say to you in all sincerity that, even though for me the experience was painful, the unfortunate demonstration on Monday had a wholesome aspect. It provided many with an opportunity to express their attachment to France and their fear of being abandoned. If that is what the immense majority of men and women at the War Memorial wanted to make known, I assure them that they have been heard. France will remain in Algeria. The bonds linking metropolitan France and Algeria are indissoluble.[12]

Mollet's first decision thereafter was to rescind his nomination of the liberal General Georges Catroux as the man to replace Jacques Soustelle as resident minister of Algeria, and to appoint instead Robert Lacoste. Henceforth, Mollet abandoned the attempt to prosecute the rebellion and to institute reform simultaneously. Rather than carry forward the fight "on two fronts," as it was called (against both the reactionary *colons* and the FLN), Mollet and Lacoste concentrated wholly on the war effort, leaving reforms to the period following the return of peace. As a result, Mendès-France resigned his cabinet post. The following year at the Congress of the Radical party, he expressed his keen sense of disappointment:

12. Speech of February 9, 1956, cited by Michael Clark, *Algeria in Turmoil: A History of the Rebellion* (Praeger, New York, 1959), pp. 285–286.

The commitments made by us during the electoral campaign have not been carried through. . . . I ask again that someone show me a single Muslim who has received a piece of land. . . . As for municipal reform, not a single right-wing mayor has been replaced either by a Muslim or a liberal Frenchman. On the administrative level, there have been many more Muslim bureaucrats chased away than hired in the last fifteen months. . . . From time to time someone tries to mislead opinion on this Algerian affair and to pretend that reforms are going on. . . . Unfortunately, the reforms have been only mystifications which have never misled the Muslim masses.[13]

Mendès-France's criticism of Mollet stands for a host of similar indictments. But how well founded are they? In essence, Mendès-France was making the same charge against Mollet that Mollet had previously made against Faure: to be successful, reform must accompany force. The questionable premise in this thinking was that the proper mix of reforms might somehow preserve Algeria for France. Thus, despite the apparent differences between Mollet and Mendès-France after the latter left the government in May 1956, on the fundamental issue the two men were actually in the same camp. For Mendès-France, like most of the non-Communist left, believed Algeria could still be made secure. Reform coupled with force could still produce the "psychological shock," a term current at the time, necessary to bring the Muslim population back to the side of France. Indeed, since 1955, there had been a veritable deluge of articles in center-left publications on the virtues of different schemes of federalism and the like. *L'Express, Esprit,* and *La Nef* regularly carried articles by prominent liberal writers and politicians proposing various vague formulas to assure the future of France abroad.[14] Mendès-France's branch of the Radical party was no exception. In 1957 it published a brochure entitled, significantly, "Save French Algeria," containing excerpts from speeches by Mendès-France, party position papers, and motions of party committees. Invariably the theme was the same: reform in order to preserve. Whatever the differences within the party ranks, these reformers shared the

13. *Le Monde,* May 4, 1957.
14. For a comprehensive review of these periodicals, see Paul C. Sorum, *Intellectuals and Decolonization in France* (University of North Carolina Press, Durham, 1977).

common illusion that the right kind of change could keep Algeria French.[15]

At first reading, the achievements of the Mollet government in relation to black Africa seem anomalous. Mollet appointed Houphouet-Boigny, a prominent leader of the RDA from the Ivory Coast, to his Cabinet and encouraged his Minister of Overseas France Gaston Defferre to draw up a framework law anticipating the future political development of French Africa. The bill, adopted in June 1956 by the National Assembly, provided for universal, single-college suffrage to local assemblies but allowed them only minimal powers. But the enabling decrees of January to April 1957 were substantially more liberal, turning local councils general into governments in embryo and providing for more prerogatives to the various assemblies than had originally been foreseen.[16] One common explanation for French initiative in this regard is that the French had learned a lesson from Indochina and were wisely applying it in black Africa. But another reading of this development is possible that reverses the line of thinking: the success of the French with reforms practiced south of the Sahara strengthened their determination that an equally positive outcome could be reached in Algeria. What they wanted to find in North Africa, that is, was someone like Houphouet-Boigny or Léopold Senghor, both loyal friends of France as well as nationalists, and a political situation as open to formative manipulation as was the case farther to the south. Here is additional evidence that Mollet genuinely intended reform, but that the situation defied his attempts to introduce change within order. The same contradiction appears implicit in Mendès-France's campaign platform of 1958. Leaflets with his picture carried an eight-point program on the back, two of which read, "Give back to France her

15. "Sauver l'Afrique française: le dossier du Parti Radical, 1955–1957," by the Parti Républicain Radical et Radical Socialiste. For example, the party's Subcommittee on Algeria passed a motion "affirming that it is out of the question, whatever the external pressures, that Algeria one day cease being French," p. 12. Again, it called for a federal formula for "a French Algeria where French sovereignty will not be questioned," p. 28. And one section is entitled, "The New Structure of a True French Union, Federalism." While the Radicals were split on many aspects of their Algerian policy, citations from Mendès-France along this line are included, p. 8.

16. Ruth S. Morgenthau, *Political Parties in French-speaking West Africa* (Oxford University Press, London, 1964), Chapter 2.

role as a Great Power" and "Make peace in Algeria."[17]

The man in power who perhaps best expressed this form of thinking (common to both Mollet and Mendès-France, whatever their differences in emphasis) was François Mitterrand. Head of the Union Démocratique et Socialiste de la Résistance (UDSR), a strategically placed center party formed in 1945 by five non-Communist Resistance groups, Mitterrand, in his capacity as minister of the colonies, negotiated a parliamentary coalition between his party and the African deputies of the RDA after the latter broke with the Communists in 1950. In 1954, Mitterrand became minister of the interior in the Mendès-France government, and so was the cabinet official in charge of Algerian affairs when the revolution started there in 1954. Again, in 1956, he was named minister of justice in Mollet's Republican Front government.

Unlike Mendès-France, Mitterrand continued to support Mollet's policies, approving his stands both on Algeria and on Suez.[18] In 1953, and again in 1957, Mitterrand published books expressing in some respects the quintessence of the liberal dilemma: he called for far-reaching change, but insisted that it be firmly under the control of Paris, And he believed that such a policy would reinforce French sovereignty overseas. As he put it in 1957, his proposal called for "a strongly structured central power in Paris, autonomous states and territories federated within an egalitarian and fraternal community whose frontiers will go from the plains of Flanders to the Equatorial forests. . . . For without Africa there will be no History of France in the twenty-first century."[19]

17. The leaflet is reproduced in Francis de Tarr, *The French Radical Party from Herriot to Mendès-France* (Oxford University Press, London, 1961). For a more extended analysis of Mendès-France similar to that presented here, see Thomas A. Cassilly, "The Anti-Colonial Tradition in France: The Eighteenth Century to the Fifth Republic" (unpublished doctoral dissertation, three vols., Columbia University, 1975), Chapter 12.

18. Roland Cayrol, *François Mitterrand, 1945–1967* (Fondation Nationale des Sciences Politiques, Paris, 1967), pp. 11ff.

19. François Mitterrand, *Présence française et abandon* (Plon, Paris, 1957), p. 237. See also the first chapter of his earlier book *Aux Frontières de l'Union française* (Julliard, Paris, 1953). Much the same case could be made against André Philip, for despite the title of his book, *Le Socialisme trahi* (Plon, Paris, 1957), he declares his faith in a federal solution between France and Algeria, pp. 181–182, 188–194.

Here, more plainly than elsewhere perhaps, the reasoning by analogy from black Africa to the case of Algeria seems evident. But the assessment of such thinking must be harsh: it was, historically speaking, pointless to wish that in Algeria in 1957, any more than in Indochina earlier, a compliant nationalist elite of Houphouet-Boigny's kind could be found. For the peaceful evolution of France's relations with the Ivory Coast differed markedly from the experience with Indochina and Algeria, not so much because of the character of French policy there but because of the character of the colonial territories where this policy was applied. Indeed, French imperial policy in the late 1940's had the same general outline everywhere: reforms were to be granted to reinforce French sovereignty; when this did not succeed, agitation against the French presence was to be repressed. Thus, from the time of the Bamako Congress of the RDA in 1946, when African political leaders seemed to be making common cause with the French Communists, until the rapprochement between Houphouet-Boigny and Mitterrand in the spring of 1950, Paris tried to destroy the RDA in French West Africa and to undermine the position of Houphouet-Boigny within the Ivory Coast. Ultimately, as is well known, Houphouet-Boigny completely changed his political tactics, recognizing that he could gain much more of what he wanted working *with* Paris rather than in opposition.

Immediately after World War II, nationalism in French black Africa was most advanced in Senegal and the Ivory Coast. But it was the Ivory Coast that quickly emerged as the key territory in French policy south of the Sahara. Here the leading political movement was Houphouet-Boigny's Parti Démocratique du Côte d'Ivoire (PDCI), which originated from the coffee and cocoa planters' voluntary association, the Syndicat Agricole Africain (SAA). As president of the SAA, Houphouet-Boigny had been elected to the French Constituent National Assembly, and there, in the spring of 1946, had proved instrumental in passing legislation to end the bitterly hated forced-labor regulations that were in effect throughout French Africa under the Third Republic and were intensified under Vichy. By this legislation, Houphouet-Boigny was able to strike a decisive blow for his own class against the European planters in coffee and cocoa (who could not compete with the Africans without the help of cheap requisitioned labor) and at the same time to enlist the support of the great mass of the territory's inhabitants who were subject to these terrible regulations. So Houphouet-Boigny, the largest planter in the Ivory Coast, became, in the words of Ruth Morgenthau "a hero and liberator. This achievement was the beginning of a myth around Houphouet, the first truly national Ivory Coast tradition."[20] By October 1946 the PDCI had 65,000 members, making it the largest party in French tropical Africa.

At the very time the Ivory Coast was securing an initial measure of national unity behind Houphouet-Boigny, the country was finding itself in increasing difficulties with the French administration. The economic aspect of the problem was familiar throughout the world at that time: shortages and inflation. But it was aggravated in the Ivory Coast by the sharp decline in world market prices for coffee and cocoa, which together constituted 75 to 92 percent of the country's exports between 1947 and 1957.[21] Meanwhile, in the Territorial Assembly, a number of political issues seriously divided the PDCI from the settler delegates and the colonial administration. What brought these local issues to the intense concern of Paris, however, was the alliance that had been growing up between the PDCI and the French Communist party, and the increasingly dominant role the PDCI was playing throughout the Federation of French West Africa (AOF).

As we have seen, in the First Constituent National Assembly (October 1945 to May 1946), the African deputies had recognized both the Socialists and Communists as their allies in the effort to secure liberal reforms in colonial rule. Although the leaders of the provisional government assured the Africans these reforms would not be modified whatever the fate of the first draft of the Constitution, the promise was not kept. In response, some 800 delegates from French Africa assembled at Bamako in October 1946 to coordinate their efforts to secure liberal reforms. In an effort to sabotage the Congress, Colonial Minister Moutet used his influence inside the Socialist party to convince Africans affiliated with his party, most notably the Senegalese, to boycott the meeting. In the absence of the well-organized Senegalese, the

20. Morgenthau, *Political Parties,* p. 181.
21. Aristide Zolberg, *One-party Government in the Ivory Coast* (Princeton University Press, Princeton, 1969), p. 163.

PDCI with Houphouet-Boigny at its head emerged as the un-rivaled leader of both French West and Equatorial Africa through the creation of the interterritorial RDA. Several years later this was to prove critically important when the issue of attaining independence as a federation arose and the unionists within the RDA found themselves cut off from their Senegalese allies outside and so less able to thwart what had come to be Houphouet-Boigny's goal of breaking the federation into sovereign states. In the immediate, a boycott on the part of the French parties that had also been invited to the Congress as observers meant that the Africans responded favorably to the one metropolitan party in attendance, the PCF. It was hardly surprising, then, that the newly formed RDA would affiliate itself with the Communists in the first legislature of the Fourth Republic elected in November 1946.

With the exclusion of the Communists from the French government the following May, and especially with the railway strikes in West Africa in the fall of 1947, Paris began to anticipate the need to deal with the same firm hand in West Africa that it had already shown in Indochina, Algeria, and Madagascar. In January 1948, Socialist deputy Paul Béchard was appointed governor general of AOF and Orselli was named governor of the Ivory Coast. When a somewhat conciliatory policy showed no signs of progress, Orselli was replaced by Laurent Péchoux, and the administration cracked down to rid the territory of the RDA by the time of the elections to the second legislature in 1951. Naturally this repression, as it was frankly called, fell most heavily in the Ivory Coast. PDCI officials were imprisoned en masse, villages favorable to the party found their taxes raised, even pilgrims to Mecca were prohibited from leaving if they were members of the party. In a move familiar in all the French territories after World War II, administrators reorganized electoral districts and rigged elections to favor hand-picked candidates. The repression did not go unanswered. Between February 1949 and January 1950 the party responded in kind to these measures. Hunger strikes, mass demonstrations, acts of civil disobedience, and actual street fighting took the lives of several score Africans while hundreds were injured and thousands arrested.[22]

22. For a review of the period see Morgenthau, *Political Parties,* pp. 188ff; and Zolberg, *One-party Government,* pp. 131ff.

For our concerns, the most striking thing about these developments is that ultimately the policy achieved its aims. Unlike the situation in Algeria or Indochina, but like the case of Madagascar, force worked. From the spring of 1950 when Houphouet-Boigny met with Mitterrand in Paris until the present day, France has had no better friend in Africa. Appearing here is the outstanding success of French decolonization, the exemplar of the policy of reform within order designed to guarantee a continued French presence overseas. It raises the obvious question of what factors were present in the case of the Ivory Coast that were lacking in Indochina and Algeria.

The most apparent problem facing Houphouet-Boigny in the period from February 1949 to January 1950 was the inadequacy of his party organization. Relative to the other political formations in French Africa, the PDCI may have seemed a potent force, but it simply could not tolerate the pressures put on it by the French administration. It should be recalled that the PDCI only came into existence in 1946, and that it built on the foundation of the SAA created just two years earlier. While it is true that the SAA associated tribal chiefs with commoners and that Houphouet-Boigny had important credentials both as a planter and as the scion of a leading chief family, this simply did not constitute strength enough to withstand the French. The root weakness of the party seems to have been the tribal structure of the country. The PDCI was in fact an "indirect party" in the sense that its structure depended more on the loyalty of elites who had their bases independent of party control than on the authority the party could muster on its own account. Beneath its upper levels, party structure mirrored rather than bridged the cleavages within the society at large. Once the top split, the party, devoid of horizontal linkages at lower levels, simply fragmented into its constituent parts. As Aristide Zolberg puts it, "the structures created in 1947 helped maintain ethnic ties even when economic and social change might have diminished their importance, . . . basic party units coincided with ethnic wards, and party life also reinforced ethnicity. . . . Those who were particularly responsible for party organization knew that its machinery was adequate only for electoral purposes."[23] What occurred under French pressure was, quite simply, the disintegration of this elite as some

23. Zolberg, *One-party Government,* pp. 143, 237.

succumbed to hopes for personal gain while others responded to fears of personal loss.

Alone, however, this cannot explain Houphouet-Boigny's capitulation to the French. Other parties at other times have been fractured by repression only to arise more powerfully thereafter. Conceivably, Houphouet-Boigny might have appealed over the head of his fellow party leaders to the people, retired to the bush, and begun a war of national liberation against the French. If a West African specialist balks at the idea, certainly a student of Asian politics would not. After all, Houphouet-Boigny was widely acknowledged to have charismatic personal qualities, and the election results after his reconciliation with France suggest that in the eyes of the people his opposition served to heighten his prestige. But this is not the course of action he chose. In a word, as the largest planter in the Ivory Coast, Houphouet-Boigny realized the obvious: the future of his class and thereby his people lay with France. Mobilize the peasantry as in Algeria? Conduct guerrilla warfare? Nothing seems less probable. As this Catholic, this traditional chief, this leading spokesman of the African bourgeoisie put it to his compatriots at the opening of a fair in 1953: "If you don't want to vegetate in bamboo huts, concentrate your efforts on growing good cocoa and coffee. They will fetch a good price and you will become rich."[24]

To promote these export crops, the Ivory Coast of the early 1950's needed the cooperation of France, for the country produced only 3 percent of the world's output—that it was of an inferior variety made it especially vulnerable to price fluctuations on the international market. Under a 1954 agreement with France, however, Ivory Coast coffee (accounting in those days for some 57 percent of total exports) received both a quota guarantee and a price floor in metropolitan markets. The growing middle class of African planters, along with their upper-class associates on the great estates, depended for their livelihood on the stability of these contracts.[25]

24. Zolberg, *One-party Government*, p. 165.

25. Elliot J. Berg, "The Economic Basis of Political Choice in French West Africa," *American Political Science Review*, LIV (1960), p. 290. In 1944, there were 40,000 of these farms. By 1956, there were 120,000 in a country whose total population was under 3 million. Coffee prices were some 20 percent above the world level. Zolberg, *One-party Government*, pp. 27, 165.

Houphouet-Boigny and the interests he represented faced another, equally serious, threat: the danger of incorporation into a federal West Africa. Since 1940, French practice had been to finance the entire Federation from indirect taxes levied throughout the area. Wealthier territories perennially complained about this practice in the Grand Council in Dakar, but to no avail. After 1945, the Ivory Coast confirmed a trend begun earlier, so that by the mid-1950's it was the undisputed economic leader of the AOF, accounting for 45 percent of the region's exports. As a result of the Federation's taxing system, however, the Ivory Coast received an average of only 19 percent of the money it remitted to Dakar. These taxes to the federal authority amounted, in turn, to two or three times the amount collected and retained locally, so that of the total governmental revenue levied in the Ivory Coast, well over half left the country never to return.[26] At the same time, the Ivory Coast was the recipient of a large influx of migrant labor from other parts of West Africa. With a strong federal structure it would have been possible for this labor force to gain significantly more political—and thereby economic—benefits than would otherwise be the case.[27]

In order to make good its separation from French West Africa, the Ivory Coast needed the support of France, for throughout the Federation in the early 1950's, the mood was for union. Houphouet-Boigny's preference for decentralization met the opposition of Léopold Senghor from outside the RDA, while Sékou Touré of Guinea began to challenge the Ivory Coast leadership from within. As a result of French support, however, Houphouet-Boigny could disregard the opinion of his fellow. West Africans. The French National Assembly's framework law of March–April 1957 severely weakened the federal authority of the AOF by removing certain of its powers to Paris and devolving others onto the reinforced territorial assemblies.

This digression to review French policy toward the Ivory Coast

26. Computed from figures provided by Zolberg, *One-party Government*, pp. 159ff.
27. Zolberg, *One-party Government*, p. 41, estimates the foreign work force at one-fourth the active population in the 1950's. The United States State Department, *Handbook for the Ivory Coast*, 1973, p. xvii, estimates this at one-third for 1970.

illuminates the key difference between this black African territory and Algeria: the nationalist elite in the Ivory Coast found
that it had much to gain from the French connection. Both
internationally (since Paris could determine the price of the export crops whose sale was crucial to this elite) and locally (since
Paris alone could protect this territory from incorporation into a
greater union), the political leaders of the Ivory Coast could be
made to see that their interests lay in cooperation with the French
in a fashion quite unlike that which existed in Algeria. Here the
French could not bargain with the same promises or threats. And
those Frenchmen, like Mitterrand, who apparently thought they
could, simply showed their ignorance by reasoning by analogy
from black Africa to the case of Algeria.

Thus, the combination of force and reformism could not gain
in Algeria (any more than in Indochina) what it achieved in black
Africa. In retrospect, then, the importance of February 6, 1956,
when Mollet visited Algiers, was not so much the tombstone it laid
at the head of reformism—this had occurred at least as long ago
as the first rigged election to the Algerian Assembly—but its
impact on certain groups in French society, particularly the settlers, the military, and various groups on the extreme right. In the
case of the European population of Algeria, for example, direct
public action had been a tradition in getting the attention of Paris
since the late nineteenth century. Generally, it was successful. In
this sense, February 6, 1956, was a dress rehearsal for May 13,
1958, when crowds would storm the government buildings in
Algiers, precipitating the fall of the Fourth Republic. More, Mollet had encouraged the settlers in their harsh interpretation of the
revolution and had promised again, as other French leaders
before him, that France would never quit Algeria. The fear and
panic that seized the settler community some five years later when
eventual French withdrawal seemed to be certain originated at
least in part in the recklessness of painting the forces of rebellion
in such lurid colors and pledging never to abandon Algeria to
such a fate.

The negotiating platform Mollet decided to adopt toward the
insurgents was his much repeated "triptych": cease-fire, free elections, negotiations. Underneath the democratic wrappings surrounding the notion of free elections, Mollet's determination to

remain in control in Algeria showed through. France would negotiate only a cease-fire with the FLN. Subsequently, three months after a "return to calm"—defined by Mollet not in military terms but as a "psychological demobilization"—elections would be held. But the elections would not be to a renewed Algerian Assembly; rather they would be to a scattering of local assemblies that in turn would determine the future status of the country. Just in case it was not clear that such a series of controls would keep Algeria French, Mollet explicitly declared that under no circumstances would independence be the final outcome.[28]

In declaring that Algeria would remain French, Mollet was able to use the rhetoric of socialism to justify repressing a popular uprising. Stressing the internationalism of his concerns, Mollet announced his conviction and that of his party that for a backward country like Algeria to prize its national identity was ridiculous:

The Socialist concern is to spare the dependent peoples the nationalist phase [of historical development]. We believe that a people can see its desire for emancipation and its will to be free from all oppressions satisfied, without at the same time giving in to a reaction of isolation and retreat which characterize nationalism.[29]

"How is it possible," Mollet asked elsewhere, that "the Algerian nationalists could be so absurd as to fight to the death in order to obtain the right to send their people back to a centuries-old misery?"[30] Employing the standard argument that France alone could bring progress to Algeria, Mollet contrasted the benefits of continued French rule to those of "an independence which would have as its certain consequence an economic and social regression and a political regression to a dictatorship or to the quasi-feudal regime of one of the Arab states. Would this be progress?"[31] His

28. Mollet's plan was frequently discussed. See *Le Monde,* January 10 and January 11, 1957; *Journal officiel,* March 27, 1957, pp. 1909–1911; and the "Motion on Algeria" voted at the 49th Congress of the SFIO in 1957, reprinted in the *Rapports* for the 50th National Congress (Bulletin intérieur, number 102, Parti Socialiste, Section Française de l'Internationale Ouvrière), pp. 133–136. By way of contrast, see the defeated motions of Gaston Defferre and Robert Verdier, pp. 136ff, the latter of which especially seems to recognize the need to negotiate the eventual independence of Algeria.

29. Mollet, *Bilan et perspectives socialistes,* pp. 45–46.

30. Mollet, *13 mai 1958–13 mai 1962,* p. 109.

31. *Journal officiel,* March 27, 1957, p. 1910.

conclusion to these rhetorical questions sounded much like those of his fellow Socialist Prime Minister Ramadier, speaking a decade earlier in regard to Indochina. As Mollet put it:

The world expects much of France, of her traditional generosity, of her daring to walk the path of great worthwhile changes. This role will be fully assumed only if we show ourselves equally daring and generous toward the peoples overseas. . . . We will show to these people who are our friends that, faithful to her liberating mission, France will lead them to freedom.[32]

In such a manner reformism became a mask for repression. For once in power, Mollet took the final steps in a logical process whose symbolically decisive moment had been the validation of the fraudulent election returns to the National Assembly from Algeria in 1951. Thus, 1944 to 1948 had been the years of naive optimism—genuine liberalism and French sovereignty would each serve the end of the other. These halcyon days ended when it became apparent that liberalism would only aid the Algerian nationalists to separate their destiny from that of France. The second period, from 1948 to 1954, offered ample proof of the contradictory character of the French ambitions in Algeria, but the evidence was steadfastly denied by a practice and rhetoric built on fraud and backed by the threat of force. With the failure of promises alone to hold Algeria, France resorted unhesitantly to force. The decisive period of the commitment to force was under Mollet.

The resort to force under the conditions of political life in the Fourth Republic meant that the government either explicitly delegated or lost to military initiative important powers held by Paris. This development was most publicly apparent in the vote of "full powers" to the government in March 1956, and their subsequent use during the liquidation of the FLN terrorist organization during the Battle of Algiers later the same year. This was only the surface manifestation, however, of a process that was coming to make Algiers, not Paris, the center of authority for the prosecution of the revolution. "Well before the Algerian uprising of May 13, 1958," writes one careful observer of the French military, "the army had been delegated full police and administrative

32. *L'Année politique*, 1956, January 31, 1956, p. 461.

powers on the local level in almost all parts of Algeria."[33] The traditional counterweight to the military hierarchy, the civilian administration, only collaborated in this development since the civil bureaucracy in Algeria had always been notorious for representing only settler interests. When Mollet appointed his fellow Socialist Robert Lacoste to the position of resident minister of Algeria (having upgraded the post of governor general), the circle was complete. Stubbornly committed to French Algeria, and a Socialist as well for good rhetorical measure, Lacoste conspired in the military's arrogation of power from Paris. Here the most flagrant case was the highjacking, accomplished without the knowledge of Paris, of a Moroccan plane carrying Ben Bella and other FLN leaders from Rabat to Tunis.[34]

Lacoste was also able to help shield the military from outside civilian investigations of torture in Algeria. As early as December 1951, Claude Bourdet, a leftist journalist and politician, had reported the use of torture in the treatment of Muslims arrested for suspected political crimes.[35] In January 1955, shortly after the outbreak of the revolution, he repeated the charge. This same year an officially designated inspector general investigated the situation in Algeria in this regard and submitted a report to Governor General Soustelle documenting numerous incidents of torture in the region he had visited and arguing that there was good reason to suppose the situation similar elsewhere.[36] Subsequently, a number of articles and books appeared providing further documentation, for the presence of the conscript army in Algeria and the experiences of the uprising in Algiers shook the cloak of military secrecy. In addition to Bourdet's articles, the more notable publications during Mollet's term in office on torture in Algeria included *Contre la torture* by the Catholic P. H. Simon, and J. J. Servan-Schreiber's serialization of his experiences as an officer in Algieria in *L'Express* (later to appear in book

33. John Ambler, *Soldiers against the State* (Anchor, New York, 1968), p. 231. See also p. 232 and notes p. 250.

34. Mollet at first hesitated, then congratulated the military on its arrest of the rebel chiefs, *Journal officiel*, October 23, 1956.

35. Claude Bourdet, "Y-a-t-il une Gestapo algérienne?" *France-Observateur*, December 6, 1951.

36. This report was kept secret until *Vérité-Liberté* published a copy in 1961 (issue number 11).

form as *Lieutenant en Algérie*). The insubordination of General
Paris de Bollardière in approving Servan-Schreiber, and the res-
ignation of the director of police in Algiers, Paul Teitgen, added
to the public notoriety of the issue.

It was not so much isolated incidents of torture that indicted the
Mollet government (although the descriptions of electric shock
treatments, beatings, forced bloating with water, and the like
were particularly appalling to a country familiar with the horror
of Nazism) but its apparently systematic use and Mollet's denial of
its existence. Its use was the outcome of the style of war being
fought, where the rebels depended for success upon their con-
cealment in the native population, whence they could emerge to
inflict lightning attacks or engage in acts of terrorism. On this
point at least, Jean-Paul Sartre and General Massu, military commander of the Algiers region, were in complete accord. As General Massu put it in an argument with General Billotte, who called
the use of torture dishonorable: "Do you believe that we can enjoy
the luxury of waiting weeks, or even days, when a bomb thrower
could give the address of the cache where the machines are?
Should hundreds die—and I mean hundreds—rather than we
dirty our hands?"[37]

In his Introduction to Henri Alleg's *La Question*, perhaps the
best-known single testimony on torture in Algeria, Sartre dismissed the moralists (such as Camus and Simon, though he mentioned no names) who denounced the act but hesitated to denounce the war and give the Algerian people their freedom:

And what is the use of troubling the conscience of the executioner? If one
of them flinched his chiefs would replace him: one lost, ten found. . . .
No, it is not enough to punish or to re-educate several individuals; no we
will not humanize the Algerian War. Torture came there of itself: the
circumstances suggested it and it was required by racist hatreds; in a
certain way, as we have seen, it is at the heart of the conflict. . . . If we
want to put an end to these sad and inhuman cruelties, to save France
from shame and the Algerians from hell, there is only one way, still the
same, the only way we have ever had, the only one we will ever have: open
negotiations, make peace.[38]

37. *Preuves*, January 1958, reprinted in *Preuves*, December 1960, p. 13. In
1971, the debate began afresh with Jacques Massu's publication of *Vraie bataille
d'Alger* (Plon, Paris, 1971), which produced a storm of criticism including Jules
Roy, *J'accuse le Général Massu* (Editions du Seuil, Paris, 1972).
38. Reprinted in Sartre, *Situations*, V, p. 88.

In the heat of this controversy, Mollet asserted that "reprehensible acts" were so few that they "could almost be counted on one's fingers."[39] On March 27, 1957, he stated before the National Assembly:

If it were true that [prisoners] were the object of torture, I declare that no excuse would be valid, even the legitimate anger born of atrocities committed against innocent victims, old people, women, children [by the FLN]. . . . I am sure, ladies and gentlemen, that none of you would do the injustice of thinking that the government, the army, or the administration might want to organize torture. . . . Cases have been cited. I must say it is rare, too rare alas, that those who bring such accusations against us agree to give sufficient evidence of place and time to permit us to seek out and identify the alleged offenders.[40]

But to pacify the critics, Mollet created a Commission for the Safeguard of Individual Rights and Liberties to investigate the situation in Algeria and clear the name of France defamed, as he put it, by a "campaign organized by the enemies of France who try to present our army and our civil administration as systematically using repressive methods contrary to the respect of the human person in Algeria."[41] Not surprisingly, the Commission encountered great difficulties in obtaining information in Algeria. Nonetheless, its final report presented ample evidence of illegal searches and detentions, mysterious disappearances, and extensive use of torture.[42] Although submitted in June 1957, the report was not made public until *Le Monde* managed to obtain a copy six months later. Mollet, then out of power, is reported to have commented on its publication: "It is true that intolerable acts have been committed in Algeria by local or metropolitan Frenchmen. . . . Did I not create the Commission whose report we want published?"[43]

In France as in Algeria, Mollet worked to keep the truth of the conduct of the rebellion from the public. He and his Defense Minister Bourgès-Maunoury (who was to succeed him as prime minister) assailed the "defeatist press" exposing the torture scan-

39. Cited in Pierre Vidal-Naquet, ed., *Raison d'état* (Editions de Minuit, Paris, 1962), p. 111.
40. *Journal officiel*, March 27, 1957, p. 1911.
41. Cited in Jean Planchais, *Le Malaise de l'armée* (Plon, Paris, 1958), p. 311.
42. Ambler, *Soldiers against the State*, p. 239; Sorum, *Intellectuals and Decolonization*, Chapter 5.
43. Cited in Planchais, *Le Malaise de l'armée*, p. 311.

dals. Mollet used financial threats against *Le Monde,* increased
radio censorship, and allowed a number of publications to be
seized for the articles they contained.[44] In late March 1957, Bourgès-Maunoury had the homes of twelve contributors to *France-
Observateur* raided and Claude Bourdet arrested on charges of
demoralizing the army. Several days later he repeated the tactic
against the home of a contributor to *Le Monde* and warned in the
Dépêche de Toulouse that he would not hesitate to prosecute those
whose words "uttered consciously or unconsciously" tended to
the demoralization of the army.[45] Correspondingly, within the
SFIO, Mollet acted to silence criticism of his policy and to oust
recalcitrant members.[46]

Not only was the evolution of Mollet's Algerian policy con-
sonant with the colonial consensus shared by the bulk of the
French political elite (and not the result of his personal character
or the style of the system as is usually suggested), but it had its
support in public opinion. A quick reading of opinion polls taken
at the time might suggest that the colonial spirit was waning in
France, since the percentage of those interviewed favoring integration with Algeria fell between October 1955 and September
1957 from 47 percent to 36 percent, while the percentage favoring "less tight bonds" between the two countries rose from 26
percent to 40 percent (with the remainder of those questioned
expressing no opinion). But as a July 1957 poll reports, the
situation was actually more complex, since those who preferred
formulas short of integration fell into two quite different groups,
one of which was obviously influenced by all the talk around the
framework law of 1957–1958, discussed in Chapter 1:[47]

Q. Among the three following solutions, which do you favor for
    Algeria?

    Treat Algeria like a group of regular French depart-
    ments, that is, that all inhabitants, Muslim or French,

44. To mention only two articles seized, both in *France-Observateur:* "Le Silence
est du sang," April 2, 1957; and "Les Jeunes soldats devant la torture," May 2,
1957.
    45. Cited in Alexander Werth, *The Strange History of Mendès-France* (Barrie,
London, 1957), p. 303.
    46. Philip Williams and Martin Harrison, *De Gaulle's Republic* (Longmans,
London, 1960), p. 41.
    47. *Sondages, Revue Française de l'Opinion Publique,* published by the Institut
français d'opinion publique, Paris, number 1, 1957, p. 41.

have rights equal to those of the French of France. 36%
Grant Algeria much internal autonomy although keeping her within the French Republic. 34%
Grant Algeria complete independence, that is, abandon Algeria completely with a more or less long delay. 18%
No opinion expressed. 12%
Similarly, although 34 percent of those interviewed in September 1957 declared that they found the Algerian claim to independence justified (as opposed to 47 percent who did not and 19 percent who did not reply), almost half this number did not find the recognition of Algeria's full independence to be a logical corollary. The polls reflect the pessimism of the French as well: even though only 18 percent of the population called for Algerian independence, 37 percent felt that French sovereignty would be ended there within ten years. But most significant in marking the breadth of the colonial consensus—and the place of the Communists outside it—were the answers to a number of questions where respondants were identified by political party (see Table 1).

This review of Mollet's Algerian policy contains no hitherto unknown facts. Nor does recognition of the existence of the colonial consensus seem to require extraordinary powers of insight into the period: the evidence is there for all to see. "The Government has never ceased to give an absolute priority to the necessities of Algeria," Mollet was cited earlier as stating at the close of fifteen months as prime minister: "Let us then reaffirm the essential and demonstrate a unanimous will that France remain present in Algeria."[48] He was correct to insist on the dedication of his government to the preservation of French Algeria. Why, then, is the system and not the policy held at fault? What was there about the colonial consensus that kept its shortcomings disguised and allowed it to persist despite the havoc it was wrecking with the French system of government (and the people of Algeria)? Military officers might prefer to blame *le système* instead of the policy since they held to a colonial presence so strongly and could use the regime as a scapegoat for their setbacks. Politicians might prefer to do the same since it exonerated them by putting the responsibility for failure on an institutional procedure. But in

48. *Journal officiel*, March 27, 1957.

Table 1. Public opinion in 1957 on the Algerian Revolution

Questions asked:	PCF %	SFIO %	Radicals %	MRP %	Independent Moderates %	Republican-Socialists URAS ARS %	Others %
The majority of Muslims:							
support the rebels	75	20	21	14	17	18	21
do not support them	11	49	49	56	50	57	25
The call for independence:							
is justified	88	34	30	27	21	23	31
is not justified	7	51	54	60	61	60	42
In Mr. Bourguiba:							
we can have confidence	54	12	15	12	8	14	12
we cannot have confidence	20	63	61	60	64	72	46
In the overseas territories France has done:							
very good work	5	28	28	22	37	32	
rather good work	23	48	51	52	43	46	
Total	28	76	79	74	80	78	
Between two extremes I would choose:							
to give independence to Algeria	89	31	43	35	19		39
to use all possible military means to crush the rebellion	2	48	41	41	58		28

Source: *Sondages, Revue Français L'Opinion Publique,* published by the Institut Français D'Opinion Publique, Paris, Number 1, 1957, pp. 42–50.

this inability to see the problem aright, something far more basic was involved. If we now have some idea of the origin of the colonial consensus, some of its terms, and some of the actions to which it prompted French officialdom, it nonetheless remains to explain its dogged persistence. To do this takes us to certain terms of the colonial consensus that were deeply but unselfconsciously held by the French political elite, ways of perceiving the problems in Algeria that had precious little to do with the reality of events there.

7 The Persistence of the Colonial Consensus

Algeria was not, of course, like any other part of the empire. Enumerating the reasons for its significance to France in material, strategic, and moral terms, de Gaulle later recalled that "in our national life, Algeria possessed an importance without comparison with that of any of our other dependencies."[1] Strategically, as has been noted, Algeria was the most vital of the overseas possessions. World War II had demonstrated its worth—when Algiers had been the provisional capital of France, protected by a moat of water less than 500 miles south of Marseilles. A more important feature was that France thought sentimentally of Algeria where a settler population of close to one million had come to make the area their home following the conquest of Algiers in 1830. Prime Minister Mendès-France recognized this special moral commitment to Algeria in his first official statement on the revolution several days after its outbreak:

[The populations of Algeria] enjoy French citizenship, are represented in Parliament, and have given, moreover, in peace as in wartime, without distinction of origin or religion, enough proof of their attachment to France, that France, in her turn, will not let this unity be put in doubt. Between them and the metropole, no secession is conceivable. This should be clear once and for all, as well in Algeria as in the metropole and abroad.[2]

1. De Gaulle, *Mémoires d'espoir*, p. 44.
2. *Journal officiel*, November 12, 1954, p. 4961.

Settler groups were quick to press their moral claim. Photographs of the time show "This is France" (*Ici la France*) splashed everywhere on the walls of Algerian cities. And at the beginning of 1962, there was the anguished "I am French" campaign for which 800,000 signatures were gathered in Algeria:

I am French. Metropolitan brother, listen to me and understand me. Forget slogans, prejudices, calumnies. Here is the truth: I am neither a fascist, nor a power-seeker, nor a doctrinaire, nor the man of a party, nor without a country. I am a citizen of the one and indivisible French Republic. As a French citizen, I do not need "self-determination." No one has the right to dispose of my French nationality or to force me to leave the land of my birth to keep it.[3]

Guy Mollet later expressed the response these appeals found among many Frenchmen: "There will be no solution to the Algerian problem so long as we have not found a way in Algeria so that the majority makes the law but this majority can not, by the law it makes, endanger the fundamental interests of individuals and minorities. This is the Algerian problem. It lies here."[4]

To many Frenchmen, particularly of the left politically, France had responsibilities to the Muslim population as well. But in their view, to acknowledge past injustices only increased the French obligation to do right in the present. And it was by no means obvious that the right course of action meant leaving Algeria to its own devices. One cornerstone of this argument was economic: the Muslim population could not survive without French support. In two short books of wide influence, Germaine Tillion, the North African ethnologist and former member of the Resistance, laid out the extent to which the Muslim community was dependent on association with France economically, corroborating thereby the findings of the official Maspetiol Commission which had declared in 1955, "Although the standard of living of most of the population is barely above the lowest known in the world, it can only be maintained by very important help from the metropole."[5] Tillion feared that the passions of war might result in the expulsion of Algerian workers from France and the with-

3. Marie-Thérèse Lancelot, *Organisation Armée Sécrète* (Fondation Nationale des Sciences Politiques, Paris, 1963), II, 35.
4. Mollet, *13 mai 1958–13 mai 1962*, p. 137.
5. *Le Monde*, September 3, 1955.

drawal of French technical know-how from Algeria. She looked forward instead to a fruitful future association of the two peoples whose cooperation alone could rescue the Muslim masses from their misery.[6]

The second line of argument against abandoning Algeria for the sake of the Muslims concerned the political character of the FLN. Its use of terror against other Muslims, its religious overtones, its affiliations with "demagogues" like Nasser, its apparent unwillingness to prove its popular mandate through democratic elections, its largely unknown leadership, all combined to make it suspect in many French eyes. How could all past French wrongdoing justify the final injury of turning the Algerian people over to this organization?

Algeria was also of some consequence to France economically. Moreover, since the debates concerning the reasons for the founding of the colonial empires have largely centered on the economic motivations involved, the role of these interests in effecting the decolonization process logically demands scrutiny. To be sure, it is generally denied that economic interests made any substantial difference in the French inability to decolonize easily (just as it is widely agreed that the Third Republic's empire was not acquired primarily for economic reasons). But the relevant figures have yet to be assembled. For our purposes, this is especially necessary in regard to Algeria.

It is important first to establish some estimate of what French colonial interests were, economically speaking. Henri Brunschwig's study, the most respected to date, of the different motivations behind French colonial expansion under the Third Republic, has concluded both that economic impetus was far from decisive and that it is doubtful (in retrospect) whether colonial expansion actually served the general interests of French development.[7] Brunschwig, however, does not discuss in any detail the function of colonial trade within the actual structure of the French economic system. Such a study might have revealed, for instance, that key sectors of the economy—pacesetters for the rest

6. Germaine Tillion, *L'Algérie en 1957; Les Ennemis complémentaires* (Editions de Minuit, Paris, 1960).
7. Brunschwig, *French Colonialism, 1871–1914*.

of the industrial sector—were heavily engaged in trade with technologically backward areas of the world and prospered from an imperialist foreign policy. Instead, Brunschwig simply relies on gross comparisons of the level of imperial trade to total French trade in order to discount the significance of the empire economically. Nor does he consider the larger framework of French reliance on trade with industrially weak territories and countries from Russia to the Ottoman Empire and China.[8] Rather, he narrowly restricts his investigation to the boundaries of the formal French empire. These two shortcomings raise legitimate doubts that he has established his case.

Moreover, his data reflect a steady rise in the importance of the overseas possessions in terms of French foreign trade statistics. In the early 1880's, the empire accounted for some 4.7 percent of French imports and absorbed 6.7 percent of her exports. By the time of World War I, these figures had risen to 9.3 percent and 11 percent respectively.[9] Following the war, these percentages continued to climb. By the early 1930's, the empire absorbed 33 percent of the exports of the metropole while providing 23 percent of its imports.[10] Except for the years of World War II and immediately thereafter, this level of trade remained relatively stationary. Figures for 1953—the last year of French Indochina and the year before the outbreak of revolution in Algeria—show the colonies receiving 37 percent of French exports while furnishing 25 percent of her imports.[11] Algeria, always France's largest colonial trading partner, accounted in 1953, for 27 percent of French imperial imports (or some 7 percent of total

8. In the case of Great Britain, for example, colonial trade declined in the nineteenth century at the same time that commerce with, and reliance on, economically backward countries increased. See Charles Kindleberger, *Economic Growth in France and Britain, 1851–1950* (Harvard University Press, Cambridge, 1964), p. 272; and Eric Hobsbawm, *Industry and Empire* (Pelican Books, London, 1968).

9. Brunschwig, *French Colonialism*, Chapter 6.

10. Girardet, "L'Apothéose de la 'plus grande France,' " p. 1089.

11. For the period 1938–1949, see *Annuaire statistique de l'Union française d'Outre-Mer*, 1939–1949, Vol. II, Part J, published by the Ministère des Finances and the Ministère de la France d'Outre-Mer. These figures correspond with those in *Annuaire statistique de la zone franc*, 1949–1955, Fascicule II, published by the Institut National de la Statistique et des Etudes Economiques pour la Métropole et la France d'Outre-Mer.

imports) while accepting 31 percent of her colonial exports (or some 11 percent of the total).[12] Nevertheless, it would be difficult to make the case that before the revolution the character of Algerian exports to France was in any respect essential to the latter's well-being. France, it should be recalled, had a broad agricultural base and therefore little use for the products imported from Algeria (over one-third of which in value was wine). Algerian industry was virtually nonexistent, and only some 13 percent of the country's mineral exports (mostly iron) found their way to France.[13] The various tables of foreign commerce I have been able to consult have been too imprecise to permit a determination of which French exports depended on Algerian markets, and to what extent, but it would seem that Algeria was indeed a rather important market for certain finished goods fabricated in the metropole.[14] As Raymond Aron has pointed out, however, was there any reason to suppose the Algerian market would suddenly disappear should the country become independent?[15] (The answer might, of course, be a qualified yes, since France had never been vigorously competitive internationally and so had relied on a protectionist empire to counter the free-trade imperialism of the Anglo-Saxons.)

Brunschwig also seems to have forgotten that trade statistics are not the only, or even the most important, measure of the economic importance of empire. As the British case pointedly illustrates, overseas investment may affect a country's economic system and international position more significantly than balance-of-payments reports alone suggest. Here the evidence is sketchy indeed and notoriously difficult to obtain. It is likely, however, that "grand capital" was more interested in Indochina,

12. *Bulletin mensuel de statistique d'Outre-Mer,* number 6, November–December 1954, published by the Ministère des Finances et des Affaires Economiques, computed from tables pp. 2, 11.

13. *Bulletin mensuel,* tables p. 10.

14. *Bulletin mensuel,* January 1954, p. 22, reports that about 50 percent of exported manufactured goods went to the empire in 1953. But in *Annuaire statistique* only a limited number of finished goods were listed as depending on colonial markets for more than 50 percent of export demand: machine motors, rubber goods, paper products, pharmaceuticals, textiles, inks, and dyes.

15. Raymond Aron, *L'Algérie et la République,* Annex 1; and *Espoir et peur du siècle* (Calmann-Levy, Paris, 1957), pp. 195ff.

Morocco, and areas of black Africa such as the Ivory Coast than it was in Algeria. But size of investment alone is no sure indicator of reaction, which would seem to have more to do with the nature of the postindependence regime than with the loss of empire *per se*. In this regard, the radical leaders of the Algerian revolution (like those in Indochina) were viewed with far more concern in Paris than were the nationalist elites in Africa south of the Sahara. Hence, there were all the French efforts to locate some other group of Muslims with whom they could negotiate in Algeria. Whatever the case, the extent and political significance of French investments in Algeria is a worthwhile question remaining to be studied. My own reading would nevertheless tend to substantiate Raymond Aron's observation:

In most of the major questions discussed in France for the past ten years, it is impossible to say what French capitalists—the great, the little, the medium, the "monopolists," or the men of the trusts—wanted. I have met several representatives of this "accursed race" and I have never known them to have a decided and unanimous opinion either on a policy to be followed in Indochina or on a policy to be followed in Algeria.[16]

To be sure, the discovery of important oil and gas reserves in the Sahara during 1956 (although anticipated for more than a decade) greatly accentuated French interest in this area. French ministers began to speak of "our Saharan oil" and to suspect that there were foreign designs afoot to acquire it.[17] In April 1957, Resident Minister Lacoste issued an important directive which read in part:

A capital event of such a nature as to modify considerably the future of Algeria and France has occurred: the discovery of extensive mineral and especially petroleum resources in the Sahara. These discoveries which are, it appears, of world importance, must confirm our country in her African vocation and justify all the more the efforts of the metropole to reintroduce calm into Algeria, which is the key to the Sahara. . . . With this, our country should recover the elements of power and independence it has been wanting for some time. With these new additions, she can retake quite naturally the place due her in Europe and in the world.[18]

16. Cited in Grosser, *La IVè République*, p. 154.
17. Alexander Werth, *The De Gaulle Revolution* (Hale, London, 1960), p. 13.
18. The text is reprinted in Michel Déon, *L'Armée de l'Algérie et la pacification* (Plon, Paris, 1959), pp. 235–236.

In January of that year, the Mollet government had seen to the creation of a so-called Communal Organization of the Saharan Regions, which sought to associate all the countries claiming part of this vast desert into a large combine to exploit its wealth together. The intent of this maneuver was apparently to persuade neighboring nations to support the French effort in Algeria or, at least, to insure France's continued importance in this area should the crisis in Algeria deepen, since an independent Algeria would claim the lion's share of the region. Finally, it was over the future status of the Sahara that de Gaulle and the Algerian nationalists had one of their most protracted differences, for the French leader temporarily tried to have certain French rights to the desert recognized in order to use it as a nuclear test site and to develop its petroleum resources.

Some case might then be made for the mobilization of economic interests behind a policy for French Algeria. Trade was important, investments did exist, and there were enormous deposits of oil, gas, and iron in the Sahara. Yet, on closer inspection, the nature of the trade seems relatively unimportant, the character of the investments remains to be demonstrated, and a broad view of the motivations behind the French decision to remain in Algeria surely would not give inordinate importance to the lure of the Sahara's natural resources. Admittedly, however, these considerations were not entirely negligible, and the radical cast of the revolution made it unlikely that an independent Algerian regime would collaborate with the French in the manner Paris might always prefer.

It remains, however, for the most adamant supporters of French Algeria to furnish some of the most telling evidence of the disinterest of the captains of French industry to the question of Algerian sovereignty. To be sure, colonial extremists dwelled endlessly on the economic importance of Algeria to France. Jacques Soustelle mentioned it repeatedly, *L'Esprit Public* published a large number of learned articles on the subject, and speakers before the Comité de Vincennes, a militant group for French Algeria, regularly invoked it. As Secret Army Organization (OAS) Colonel Antoine Argoud put it in his book on Algeria: "For primary goods, the West is largely tributary to the Third World, and in particular to the ex-colonial countries. . . . One can thus state that the Western economy cannot live isolated and that any weakening of economic ties with the former colonies, and even more strongly their passage into the Communist camp, would strike it a serious blow."[19]

Such statements notwithstanding, one could scarcely call the movement to maintain French Algeria the tool of French capitalism. As Emmanuel Beau de Loménie hotly insisted in 1957, French financial and industrial interests were unpatriotically betraying France and the empire by seeking their own gain regardless of the fate of the nation.[20] So, too, Colonel Argoud often equated the twin enemies of the OAS as international communism and international capitalism. Similarly, the main publication of the OAS-CNR (Conseil National de la Résistance), *France Presse-Action* (first appearing in the spring of 1962), carried its capsule program in a small box on the front page of each edition where it included the pledge that it was "as opposed to big capitalism as to international communism." Other articles and leaflets made familiar fascist and Poujadist appeals to protect the workers and "natural communities" from capitalist spoliation and from the Jews. As one typical OAS statement declared: "The OAS fights . . . for the improvement of the standard of living of workers subservient to capitalist trusts and the Rothschild Bank which by its director Pompidou governs our country."[21] An issue of the clandestine metropolitan newspaper *Maquis-Résurrection-Patrie* expressed this with special force:

The moment has come to tell you what we will do if it pleases God to reward our faith and our good will by giving us victory: we will hang all the traitors; we will defend the Fatherland; we will assure social justice. . . . The program is large, it may appear difficult, but . . . this is the price if we are to save everything, God willing, from Communist enslavement and capitalist domination.[22]

---

19. Antoine Argoud, *Le Problème algérien: solution française* (OAS, 3éme Section: Bureau d'Etudes, clandestine, n.d.), p. 18. And see his similar comments in *Sans commentaire*, edited by the Comité Maurice Audin (Editions de Minuit, Paris, 1960), pp. 1, 26, 83.

20. Emmanuel Beau de Loménie, *L'Algérie trahie par l'argent: réponse à M. Raymond Aron* (Editions Etheel, Paris, 1957), especially pp. 52ff.

21. *OAS parle* (anonymous) (Julliard, Paris, 1964), p. 281.

22. Letter Number 6, dated June 1, 1961, from the loose-leaf collection of OAS material at the Bibliothèque Nationale, Paris.

It would seem, therefore, that economic factors were substantially more important in raising up nationalist forces against French rule in Algeria (as we saw in Chapter 4) than in influencing the way Paris would respond to this challenge.

But more than economic interest, or strategic considerations, or the moral claims of the settler and Muslim populations, was the image France had of herself that made the loss of Algeria so difficult to contemplate. Unwilling to place her future security wholly within an alliance dominated by the United States and dependent on German industry and arms, France maintained a view of international affairs in which the principal units were—or at least sought to be—sovereign nation-states. Under these terms, France without an empire would fall to the level of a third rank power. So Prime Minister Mendès-France was firm in ordering repression of the Algerian insurrection:

You can be certain, in any case, that on the part of the government there will be neither hesitation, nor evasion, nor half-measures in the arrangements it will make to assure security and respect for the law. There will be no sparing of sedition, no compromise with it: everyone here and there should know this. One does not compromise when it is a question of defending the internal peace of the nation, the unity, the integrity of the Republic. The Algerian departments constitute a part of the French Republic. They have been French for a long time and are so irrevocably. . . . Never will France, any government, any parliament, whatever its particular tendencies, give in on this fundamental principle.[23]

Edgar Faure, who succeeded Mendès-France as prime minister, renewed the pledge:

The entire honor of France as well as her human mission oblige us absolutely, without equivocation and without reticence, to keep Algeria for France and in France. Everyone at home and elsewhere must understand that we find ourselves here before a vital imperative, that any government will necessarily have as its first duty to keep France on both shores of the Mediterranean. Without Algeria and without French Africa, what would become of our country? Her economy gravely menaced, her world-wide influence compromised, she would be no more than a reflection dimming daily of her former greatness.[24]

23. *Journal officiel,* November 12, 1954, p. 4961.
24. Cited in *Combat,* September 26, 1955. See also his statements before the National Assembly, *Journal officiel,* October 13, 1955, pp. 5093ff.

Mollet, who in turn succeeded Faure, similarly rejected any possibility that France would "abandon". Algeria as "an unacceptable solution for France which would become a diminished power of second or third rank, shorn of her world role."[25]

With the moral enthusiasm born of the Resistance as well as with the practical realism born of the defeat, France sought immediately after World War II, as we have seen, to reinforce her domination overseas by evidence of a new spirit of reform. De Gaulle set the example of how to conduct a policy, showing that France must act firmly and not just generously, that although change was necessary, it would be effective in preserving French rule only where there was a sure sense that the French presence would be maintained. The optimism characteristic of the times assumed that this happy marriage of sovereignty with liberality would be an enduring partnership. Renewal in imperial relationships would parallel renewal domestically. The Jacobin spirit in France revived. Once more national and international duty coincided: continued sovereignty abroad called for reform, while reform, properly administered, would contribute to the maintenance of sovereignty. The honeymoon period from 1944 through the first months of 1946 showed some impressive accomplishments. Public authorities checked the worst of past abuses and took the first concrete steps toward recognizing and encouraging the political maturity of the colonial peoples. The leaders of France subsequently demonstrated their loyalty to de Gaulle's injunction to be firm in colonial matters as well. Between August 1946 and August 1947, they made this clear most notably to the Vietnamese at Fontainebleau and Haiphong, to the Moroccans with General Juin, to the black Africans meeting at Bamako, to the Madagascans with the repression of April 1947, and to the Algerians by the tone of the new Statute of Algeria.

Increasingly, after the end of 1946, however, it became apparent that the union of realistic self-interest and liberalism could not last. In the key areas of Indochina and Algeria, nationalist forces meant for their lands to be independent and would only turn the freer conditions created by reform to the pursuit of this end. Not de Gaulle's departure from power, but the inability of his formula

25. Mollet, *Bilan et perspectives socialistes*, p. 59.

for change to contain colonial nationalism posed a new dilemma for the French. Should they continue with reform, although now with a view to granting eventual self-government under conditions as favorable to French interests as possible? Or should they repress this agitation and try to prepare the terrain in such a manner that reform would serve their continued presence? In choosing the latter alternative in Indochina and Algeria, the French changed the terms of their colonial engagement from "we must be liberal in order to be sovereign" to "we must be sovereign in order to be liberal." In regard to Indochina, this fateful decision was reached at Fontainebleau in the summer of 1946; it was sanctioned by Blum that December, and was codified by Ramadier in the first months of the following year. In relation to Algeria, the first rigged elections in the spring of 1948 officially registered the same decision.

But surely, one might say, this is a familiar historical development whose logic can scarcely be credited to the shortcomings of some so-called colonial consensus. French national interest could rationally be seen as resting with the preservation of the empire, while French rhetoric was merely a convenient disguise for making such realism palatable to an age demanding moral platitudes. As de Gaulle remarked of Roosevelt's moralistic enthusiasm concerning the future United Nations on the occasion of one of their wartime meetings: "It was a permanent system of intervention that he intended to institute by international law. . . . I listened to Roosevelt describe his plans to me. As was only human, his will to power cloaked itself in idealism."[26] But only the politically naive would confuse why the French behaved as they did with their own declarations about it. Behind the smokescreen of reformism crouched French national interest.

What such an explanation ignores, however, is the blind spots, the misperceptions, and the rigidity of outlook that characterized the French reaction to the Algerian uprising. Whatever the rationality and realism of the French policy toward the revolution, the heart of the matter will not be exposed so long as French behavior is understood simply as having been based on rational self-interest.

26. De Gaulle, *The Complete War Memoirs*, pp. 573–574.

Twentieth-century governments must claim to be democratic in order to be considered legitimate. Hence they typically represent uprisings against their rule as the work of a handful of agitators whose actions are foreign to the needs and wishes of the general population. Repression is justified by the same token. One would then anticipate that French authorities would insistently deny a popular base to the Algerian insurrection.

But there is solid evidence to conclude that this allegation was not entirely cynical. As the Suez invasion during the fall of 1956 reveals so well, the French genuinely felt that foreign machinations were at the root of colonial discontent. Nor were they totally incorrect. London had been instrumental in evicting France from the Levant in the immediate aftermath of World War II, and Roosevelt's opposition to the colonial ambitions of Paris was common knowledge.[27] In regard to North Africa, America looked especially threatening since Roosevelt was widely reported to have encouraged the Sultan of Morocco in his claims against Paris during the Casablanca conference. Furthermore, the Algerian nationalists had initially submitted their Manifesto calling for independence not to French but to Allied authorities in Algiers; and, again, when the French planned their return to Indochina, Washington had refused to transport their troops. It is possible, nevertheless, to exaggerate the importance of these outside influences, as French public opinion surely did when the question arose as to the causes for disturbances in French territories in 1945. According to a poll taken in May 1945, 65 percent of the French people believed that the current troubles in the Levant were British inspired, while only 3 percent laid them to French causes and 2 percent to Arab initiation. Similarly, in October 1945, public opinion felt in its great majority (63 percent) that the difficulties in Indochina came from outside meddling, while only 5 percent felt the French were responsible and another 5 percent looked to the Vietnamese themselves.[28] Thus, in the case of relations with Washington, anti-Americanism flared each time France's dependent role became evident: over the Marshall Plan,

27. De Porte, *De Gaulle's Foreign Policy*, passim; Marshall, *The French Colonial Myth*, Chapters 3 and 4.

28. The polls are reported in Sorum, *Intellectuals and Decolonization in France*, Chapter 1.

the European Defense Community, the "nuclear shield," and American funds for the war in Indochina.[29]

Surely, a part of the reason Great Britain decolonized more easily than France was that London did not feel the distance from Washington that Paris felt so acutely. The different relationships Roosevelt maintained with de Gaulle and Churchill during the War illustrate the point. "He hates de Gaulle with such fierce feeling that he rambles almost into incoherence whenever we talk about him," Cordell Hull reported of Roosevelt in the summer of 1944.[30] With the North African landing of November 1942, and the assassination of Jean-François Darlan a month later, the Americans moved to make General Henri Giraud, and not de Gaulle, head of civilian administration there and commander of the surrendered French army of several hundred thousand men. Despite de Gaulle's ability in 1943 to rally behind him the National Liberation Committee (CFLN) and the support of certain resistance groups operating inside France, the Americans continued to oppose his leadership. Even at the moment of the liberation of France, Roosevelt refused to recognize the General's authority, insisting instead that a military administration run the country until the wishes of the population were made known by elections. It was October 1944 before the United States finally recognized de Gaulle's provisional government.

Certainly more than personality factors were at play. For the features of de Gaulle's personality that the Americans and sometimes the British found so antipathetic had to do with his determination not to let France be absorbed by her allies during the war or be relegated to a satellite role and deprived of all initiative thereafter. So, early in the struggle, he had protested the manner in which the British occupied Diégo-Suarez on Madagascar and conducted operations against the Vichy troops in Syria. Similarly, the General had intimations of Roosevelt's plans for the French empire: that Indochina or Morocco might be made trusteeships of other powers; that British or American bases might perma-

29. See, for example, Raymond Aron, *Immuable et changeante,* p. 234; Grosser, *La IVè République,* pp. 17, 47ff; Elgey, *La République des illusions,* pp. 101, 133, 139–141, 248; Claude Paillat, *Vingt ans qui déchirent la France: Le Guepier* (Robert Laffont, Paris, 1969), Chapters 1 and 2.

30. Cited in Gabriel Kolko, *The Politics of War: The World and United States Foreign Policy* (Random House, New York, 1968), p. 83.

nently be established on New Caledonia or at Bizerte and Dakar; even that a new buffer state might be created between France and Germany, to be called Wallonia and to run from Switzerland to the Channel.

By contrast, relations between Great Britain and the United States were far more trusting. The "special relationship between the British Commonwealth and Empire and the United States," as Churchill labeled it in his famous Fulton, Missouri, speech of March 1946, stretched far back in time. One might date its inception as 1823, when the British celebrated the Monroe Doctrine as a policy well suited to support Pax Britannica in Latin America; or in the middle of the nineteenth century, when Britain acquiesced in American pre-eminence over an eventual isthmus canal and thereby surrendered naval supremacy in the Caribbean; or at the end of the century, when Washington's Open Door Notes lent their support to the British scheme of things in China; or again at the Washington Naval Conference of 1921, when the British finally accepted parity with the United States in naval power and moved away from their alliance with Japan in the Far East. Whatever the date, the point is that London looked upon an international order maintained by Washington with some degree of optimism.

At times the British had reason to find the relationship quite frustrating. To most Britishers, it appeared that the United States would have its own way at every turn, insistent on its rights but reluctant to honor its obligations. America's power, geographic isolation and (as the sentimental liked to feel) immaturity in foreign affairs combined to produce the mixture of righteousness and irresponsibility that the British found so taxing. But it was only a minority who argued, as some radical American historians do today, that Washington's moves were in fact premeditated efforts to sap British power in a design to replace her in international affairs. As Max Beloff writes, "The degree to which British statesmen and diplomats expected a natural sympathy for British policy to exist in the United States and equated any hostility to or criticism of Britain with treason to America and not merely to Britain can be abundantly illustrated."[31] Surely the

31. Max Beloff, "The Special Relationship: An Anglo-American Myth," in Martin Gilbert, ed., *A Century of Conflict, 1850–1950: Essays for A. J. P. Taylor* (Hamish Hamilton, London, 1966), p. 156.

confidence with which Britain relied on American power after 1945 is remarkable, especially when compared with the French attitude. The ease, one might almost say the grace, with which the United States replaced Britain in Greece and Turkey in 1947 is perhaps the outstanding illustration of this "special relationship." The contrast with France is striking.

But more than Washington or London, Paris feared Moscow. For the Russians were, in a sense, located inside France in the person of the French Communist party, which in turn was connected to Communist parties throughout the empire. No sooner had the PCF formed in 1920, than it found itself accused of fomenting unrest in overseas France. By 1925, the support of the party for Abd el-Krim in his struggle against the combined French and Spanish armies in the Rif could be cited as proof positive that local disorders were of Communist instigation. Even liberal Governor General Viollette declared that by his censorship and imprisonment of Communists he would be sure that he did not "deliver Algeria to the delegates of the Third International." So Albert Sarraut declared (when he was minister of the interior in 1927 and so responsible for Algerian affairs during the Rif War): "Communism, that is the enemy."[32] As a leading expert on colonial opinion during the interwar years put it (a man few would suspect of sympathy for the Communists):

The constant identity established between the cause of colonial grievances and the cause of proletarian revolution could only lead opinion . . . to confuse systematically the imperatives of imperial defense with those of the "anti-Bolshevik struggle." The inevitable result was thereby to furnish an admirable alibi to the good colonial conscience of the masses which consolidated its prejudices and its intellectual and moral comfort. . . . Did the pre-eminent importance accorded this danger from without not contribute to the dissimulation of certain perils or problems strictly internal, born of the very evolution of the colonial societies?[33]

After the World War II and the outbreak of the Cold War, it was only a matter of time before local nationalist claims would be laid to Communist machinations. In a speech in Algiers in October 1947, while campaigning for upcoming municipal elections, Charles de Gaulle officially introduced the charge:

32. Cited in Nouschi, *La Naissance du nationalisme algérien*, pp. 58–60.
33. Girardet, "L'Apothéose de la 'plus grande France,'" pp. 1106–1107.

Of course it is in French Africa that the separatists [i.e., the Communists] carry out their greatest efforts at dislocation. This is easily explained: if France finds herself absorbed on the other side of the Mediterranean by the greatest difficulties possible, if she is divided on the manner to parry them, if she loses before these populations a part of her prestige, she would be diminished thereby, all the less able in consequence to face up to her difficulties within and without. . . . Thus we see quite well why the party of national dislocation makes our Algeria and the French Union essential objects of its evil action. We see why the bad apostles work to aggravate the multiple difficulties which arise here as everywhere.[34]

The theme was to recur: Guy Mollet, for example, in defending his invasion of Suez before the National Assembly, likened Nasser to Hitler and exposed Nasser's designs on Algeria—which made Nasser in turn a pawn of the Soviets. Mollet warned:

If France were, in effect, to abandon Algeria, leaving it to civil war, that would signify not only the departure of France from all of Africa, but the loss of Africa and its opening to the Soviet Union. (Applause left, center, right.) Thus, the USSR, which already threatens to outflank the Atlantic forces via the Near East could encircle [Europe] via Africa.[35]

What separated extremist French colonialists from their brethren in the center and center-left parties was not so much their making communism the scapegoat for colonial unrest but the singleminded insistence with which they developed this theme and those that alleged Nasser's responsibility. Even within French Algerian circles, certain groups like the so-called *intégriste* Catholics developed the notion of a terrifying Communist menace.[36] Other proimperial civilians discussed the topic ceaselessly in the pages of the weekly *L'Esprit Public*.[37] The military, for its part, set up a special administrative division to specialize in counterinsurgency. This "Fifth Bureau," as it was named, studied the

34. De Gaulle, *Dans l'attente*, p. 131.
35. *Journal officiel*, December 20, 1956.
36. M. Maître, "Le Catholicisme d'extrême droite et la croisade anti-subversive," *Revue Française de Sociologie*, II, 2, 1961. Publications of this group included Bernard Lefevre, *Sur le chemin de la restauration. Contre-révolution: Stratégie et tactique* (1958); Colonel Château-Jobert, *Manifeste politique et sociale;* and the newspapers of Robert Martel's Mouvement Populaire 13, *Doctrine* and *Travail Libre.*
37. Jean Brune's lead article, February 24, 1961, is typical of many. The headline reads "The Third World War Has Begun in Algeria" while in subtitles: "The West Has No Sword" (a reference to the bourgeoisie's lack of ideological discipline), and "Mr. K: 'The Algerian War Is a Sacred War.' "

tactics of guerrilla warfare first formulated by Mao Tse-tung and adapted by the Vietminh against the French in Indochina. The military came to the conclusion that the Communists had found a way of eroding the strength of the West by side-stepping the nuclear stalemate through a sophisticated form of internal subversion. The organizational genius Lenin had displayed when he took over Rušsia with a handful of followers had been skillfully wrought into a method suitable for exporting revolution throughout the preindustrial world. "People's Wars" were thus not authentic wars of national liberation, but insurrections masterminded from Moscow. The misery of the colonial peoples was being unscrupulously exploited by those whose ultimate ambition was the extension of their own totalitarian rule. A great many of the military's top officers developed this general theme with their own particular nuances. One of its more striking presentations appeared in a discussion outline prepared by the Fifth Bureau for the use of specially recruited speakers who would appear before civilian and military groups to discuss the character of the struggle in Algeria. The Bureau recommended that the speaker explain it in terms of this general format:

Algeria, world stake: the Russians, leaders of Communism and of world satellization, leaders of total, universal, and permanent revolutionary warfare, want to tear Algeria from France and conquer Europe as well as Africa by encirclement, and by the Atlantic, America, beginning from the South until the complete realization of the only goal fixed for thirty years: to communize and satellize the free world.

Quote Lenin: the route from Moscow to Paris passes by Pekin (1921). Make the young understand the profound meaning of this phrase: resolution, determination, declaration of war. Make them follow the successive stages of the path already followed: China, Korea, Indochina, Indonesia, India, Lebanon, Egypt, Syria, the FLN (now in contact).

Recall the dates, show the advance of the enemy on the map. Algeria, the Free World's final line before the communist invasion.

Insist on the key position of France, nation-leader of Europe, whose road, from Paris to Brazzaville, passes through Algiers. France: torch of liberty. Paris: center of world culture, final stake in the long struggle undertaken by Moscow.[38]

38. Taken from a large loose-leaf collection of Fifth Bureau material on file at the Bibliothèque Nationale, Paris. The maps referred to in the text were a common lecturing device, inevitably using phallic arrows to show the advance of world communism. For a more detailed discussion of the Fifth Bureau, see M.

It is sometimes suggested that such ideas were the province of a fanatic minority dedicated to the preservation of French Algeria. But, as we have seen, the theme had a pedigree more than thirty years old in France and was not restricted to the far right. Nor was it unique to France. Any number of American academics and politicans developed the same general world view (dubbed by President Dwight Eisenhower the Domino Theory), first in regard to the fall of China, then with respect to Indochina. In retrospect it is easy (and tempting) to credit the notion that Communist intrigues lay at the origin of popular uprisings in the Third World to a few Cold War extremists and so to forget what common currency the idea had. Thus, in the case of Algeria, Cairo was manipulating the FLN—just as Ho Chi Minh had earlier been an "advance man" for the Chinese, at least according to the United States State Department chief intelligence officer.[39]

The result was Suez. The high-blow justifications, the transparent lies, the irony of a Socialist government commandeering an expedition in defense of this sacred enclave of capitalist imperialism throw into sharp focus the unreality of French thinking about Algeria. For as General Maurice Challe, leader of the French forces into Egypt in the fall of 1956, later attested, Paris "sought the conclusion of the Algerian problem at Suez." Suez, he insisted, was "an episode linked to Algeria both in timing and strategy, by its motives and consequences."[40] According to Prime Minister Mollet, the fundamental rationale of the French action was "an anti-Munich reflex" which, he claimed, was common to the majority of Frenchmen faced with the menace of Nasser.[41] An interesting report produced at the time by Herbert Luethy and David Rodnick corroborates Mollet's testimony, finding that a

---

Megret, *L'Action psychologique* (Fayard, Paris, 1959); Ambler, *Soldiers against the State*, pp. 336ff; George Kelly, *Lost Soldiers* (M.I.T. Press, Cambridge, 1965), pp. 109ff. As the Ambler and Kelly books show, however, the ideas of the Fifth Bureau had general currency among the French military at the time.

39. See Roger Hilsman's Introduction to General Vo Nguyen Giap, *People's War, People's Army* (Praeger, New York, 1962), p. xvi. American writing in this vein is tremendous. To cite but one example, Douglas Pike, *Viet Cong: The Organization and Techniques of the National Liberation Front of South Vietnam* (M.I.T. Press, Cambridge, 1969).

40. Maurice Challe, *Notre révolte* (Presses de la Cité, Paris, 1968), pp. 18, 21.

41. *Journal officiel*, December 20, 1956.

considerable number of his countrymen agreed that to end the troubles in Algeria they must first settle with the Egyptians. Socialist Resident Minister of Algeria Lacoste summed up this mood: "One French division in Egypt is worth four in North Africa."[42]

However much the French colonial consensus might attribute the *outbreak* of the Algerian uprising to foreign machinations and the actions of a fanatic Muslim minority, it lay the responsibility for the insurrection's *perseverence* to a wholly different party: the Fourth Republic. We have arrived at the heart of the colonial consensus, the conviction that French decadence was responsible for the loss of overseas empire. And so the colonies must be held, for to acquiesce in the termination of empire, especially in the loss of Algeria, would be the final symptom of a national loss of virility which had haunted the French political mind since the defeat of 1870.

The logic of this position grew from the lessons a generation of Frenchman had learned from the bitter experiences of the thirties, World War II, and Indochina. Time and again, weak and divided governments had not faced up to outside challenges, and the country had suffered humiliating defeat. Hence the prevalence throughout the life of the Fourth Republic of appeals to Frenchmen to unite, to will victory in order that it be theirs. No theme was repeated more insistently after World War II, and no image the French had of themselves was more basic to the persistence of the colonial consensus.

Addressing the Constitutional Commission of the Second Constituent Assembly, Socialist Colonial Minister Moutet expressed this sentiment clearly: "Does France truly consider herself as uniting 110 million souls, or rather does she wish to retire into herself, considering herself only as a people of 40 million? Will France be a great power or will she not?"[43]

As the crises in the empire multiplied, so did the appeals to the force of will to overcome greater odds. Perhaps nowhere was this

42. Herbert Luethy and David Rodnick, *French Motivations in the Suez Crisis*, mimeographed (International Social Research Organization, Princeton, 1956). Lacoste is cited in Grosser, *La IVè République*, p. 370.
43. *Journal officiel*, August 27, 1946, p. 259.

more pathetically expressed than in the words of the greatly respected old governor general of Algeria, Maurice Viollette, speaking late in 1953 of the possibility of negotiations with Ho Chi Minh: "I protest with all my energy against actions so humiliating—I was going to say so shameful. . . . I am afraid, and I begin to ask myself—and this would be serious—if perhaps what France lacks is not the dynamism of the French (*l'élan des Français*)."[44] In short, from eight years of struggle in Indochina the main lesson most Frenchmen had learned was to trust themselves still less: it was not the decision to return to Indochina that was held at fault for the defeat there, but the inept system that attempted to implement this policy.

Hence alongside the determination that Algeria in its turn would not be lost was the fear that in fact it would be, and for the same reason that Indochina had been such a disaster: the shortcomings of the Fourth Republic. "The victory is more than half won," declared Socialist Resident Minister Lacoste on May 8, 1958. "It will be certain the day when those who lead France understand that there is no longer any room for the pessimists— the 'willful pessimists'—and show an unhesitant determination, clearly expressed despite the incomprehension of our allies."[45] And again:

Confidence, that is the key word of this summer of 1957. . . . If we should falter, if the French by their behavior, their attitude, their statements, allow it to be believed that a tired France is refusing the effort imposed upon her, is betraying her duties by desertion, then we will see our adversaries renew their hopes, their intrigues, their efforts, and multiply their crimes.[46]

The most resolute partisans of French Algeria ceaselessly projected this image of the nation. "The greatness of a country is indivisible," wrote Jacques Soustelle, noted scholar of pre-Columbian America, close associate of General de Gaulle, governor general of Algeria from early 1955 until February 1956, parliamentarian, and brilliant polemicist in the defense of French

44. *Journal officiel,* October 27, 1953, p. 4601.
45. André Debatty, *Le 13 mai et la presse* (Armand Colin, Paris, 1960), p. 44.
46. Cited in Ambler, *Soldiers against the State,* p. 197. Perhaps this showed the influence of the Fifth Bureau, one of whose slogans was "Pour Vaincre, il faut Convaincre."

Algeria. "It is at once that of its universities, its literature, its art, its diplomacy, its army, its industry."[47] Thus, the end of France as a "Eurafrican power" meant the end of France as "a power, period." He continued:

Algeria lost . . . would equal in depth and consequence the most horrible defeats in our history. . . . . It is clear that if France lets herself be backed into a situation where she is led to abandon Algeria, it is not only Algeria which would be lost, it would be Africa. And in losing Africa, France would lose at the same time her future.[48]

What is so remarkable about Soustelle's words—and what makes him perhaps the most instructive thinker on the tormented mind of France during this period—is not so much his extremism and vituperation as the reception that was given to important aspects of his diagnosis throughout the ranks of his countrymen. For the most telling element of Soustelle's argument was not simply that the loss of Algeria would remove France definitively from the ranks of the great powers, but that this decline would be the result of her own doing:

In reality, the drama is not that of Algeria. It is that of decadence. . . . To abandon Algeria is to condemn France to decadence; to save Algeria is to call a halt to this terrible process of degradation, to return to our country, to its people, to its youth their chance and their future.[49]

Not the connivances of the Anglo-Americans, not the Moscow-Cairo connection, but the decadence of the Republic was the fundamental factor separating Algeria from France.

Analysis of the political images generated by the colonial extremists shows none more common than those depicting the defenders of empire as masculine, tough, decided, and heroic, while the leaders of the Fourth Republic appear flabby and effete. In juxtaposition to the Fourth Republic's lack of self-confidence, the defenders of French Algeria ceaselessly projected their own crusading spiritualism and selfless dedication.[50] The point is key,

47. Jacques Soustelle, *Le Drame algérien et la décadence française: réponse à Raymond Aron* (Plon, Paris, 1957), p. 65.
48. *Journal officiel,* March 9, 1956, pp. 787–788.
49. Soustelle, *Le Drame algérien,* pp. 66, 69.
50. The trials of those officers accused of sedition are particularly replete with heroic posturing. See among others *Les Procès des Généraux Challe et Zeller* (Nou-

for far too often their fellow Frenchmen seemed to give their assent, fearing that these accusers in giving voice to their own most secret fears might be right, that a "nation of cowards" was indeed losing the glorious heritage of France. The examples of the thirties, World War II, and Indochina were there for all to see. Catastrophe had come from a divided paralyzed government that was unable to provide the leadership the country so desperately needed. And it was happening once again. Government crises, incessant quarreling when a decision needed to be reached, errors committed, acts undone—the responsibility for the debacle in Algeria could seemingly be pinpointed squarely on a system of rule, and from there to an entire people. As Mollet put it in describing the popular reaction to the military insurrection against civilian authority—when it finally occurred in 1958:

The police, army, and administration were in rout. Organize this vast and profound reaction? Of course this is what we wanted to do. Throughout an entire night, representatives of the free labor unions came through my office. The result of our consultations was clear: the working class, not because of softness but because of incomprehension, would stay quiet. They were not ready to fight for this disqualified form of government, this impotent Republic.[51]

Thus, as Mollet saw it (from a viewpoint that exonerated him from the Algerian disaster), the cause of the Fourth Republic's difficulties was not *his* policy and the colonial consensus which it embodied, but the character of the regime, "this disqualified form of government, this impotent Republic."

---

velles Editions Latines, Paris, 1961). Civilian supporters made similar appeals. See, for example, Jacques Soustelle, *L'Espérance trahie* (La Table Ronde, Paris, 1962); and Raoul Girardet, *Pour le tombeau d'un capitaine* (Editions de l'Esprit Nouveau, Paris, 1962). After the loss of Algeria, Girardet could write that "Algeria represented to France a great workyard to be opened, a new field of action for the generosity, the energy, and the creative ambitions of several generations. It was not a mediocre dream, after all, this great challenge thrown at misery, this vast collective adventure which, from the North Sea to the mountains of Hoggar, would try to establish the basis for a new fraternity. Our people would at last escape from their closed introspection, from their old, abrasive quarrels, from their tenacious, narrow, petit-bourgeois egoism. We had found our 'West.' The hour of pioneers had sounded once again. . . . Can a people live without a dream, and what other will replace the great Algerian dream? Will France of the hexagon be other than a moral and ideological void?"

51. Mollet, *13 mai 1958–13 mai 1962*, p. 97.

The rebels knew that the governments of the Fourth Republic were particularly fragile; they counted, moreover, not only on the fatigue and the discouragement of our people, but also on the moral aid, if not material, that they were accorded by the Communists and a number of naive partisan propagandists. For my part, I believe that nothing did so much as these internal divisions among the French to reinforce the most intransigent among the FLN.[52]

France in the postwar period was a nation whose leaders were morbidly preoccupied with power. Socialist concerns in this respect were little different from those of the majority of their fellow countrymen. German power had humiliated them, British and American power had doubted them, Soviet and Egyptian power then threatened them. But, especially, their own lack of power tormented them. The French had determined on a rebirth of national greatness as a means to assuage the pain of surrender and occupation, but behind the bravado of their move, the French feared their own impotence. This sensitive point was not forgotten by the enemies of Mollet's regime—de Gaulle as well as the military-colonialist alliance—who exploited it on every possible occasion.

Here, then, was the aspect of the colonial consensus which more than any other accounts for its persistence. Reversals when they came were not seen in terms of the developments within the colonial society or as growing from the character of the postwar order, so much as they were seen as reflections of French inadequacy. Algeria's loss or preservation was not, therefore, an end to be weighed against the means to secure it or against other ends. It was, in the language of the times, France's "last chance," upon which would be founded her salvation or fall, a stake of unique and final importance, closed to bargaining. To submit to "defeat" in North Africa would solve nothing, since this would only feed the national failing and aggravate the very causes of failure. The moral seemed clear: French defeats were largely self-inflicted; to reverse the course of events, France must pull herself together and win. Here was a fatal pattern of interpreting events, for the French could not learn from experience *since the lessons of history only reconfirmed their misperceptions.* Colonial confrontations in general—but particularly in Algeria—became a testing ground

52. Mollet, *13 mai 1958–13 mai 1962*, p. 87.

where the French felt called upon to prove themselves and where they risked confirming their own bad image by failing once again. The process had a self-aggravating logic, with each setback preparing the way for the next. It was like fighting quicksand—each effort to right the course of history only made it all the more difficult to control.

8 *The Definition of Withdrawal*

The great power status of France, and more importantly her image or identity as a nation, had thus come, by the middle of 1957, to hinge on the outcome of the Algerian conflict. At such a moment, only General de Gaulle possessed the ability both to make the break with Algeria and to do so in a manner that would not poison the political atmosphere of the country for more than a generation with humiliation and mutual recriminations. That Algeria today is such a relatively minor issue in French politics comes in large measure from the way de Gaulle isolated and discredited his opponents while at the same time rallying the mass of his countrymen to a new vision of themselves in the world. With bold policy initiatives on matters relating to the Atlantic Alliance, European unity, and Eastern Europe, the General restored a sense of his country's international importance. As for Algeria, he achieved what the Fourth Republic had lost all hope of doing by 1957: by granting independence he maintained (indeed even increased by some accounts) the self-respect of his people.

A man of the General's stature has commanded a great deal of attention, and there is no reason to attempt to duplicate here what others have already said of him. A few words of comment may nevertheless throw added perspective on the troubles, systemic and psychological, of the Fourth Republic by recalling the logic of the argument with which de Gaulle gave Algeria her independence and refashioned the French self-image.

To suggest, as some do, that when the General entered office he had already decided to grant Algeria independence is faithful neither to the historical record nor to de Gaulle's style as a statesman. As Stanley Hoffmann describes his political artistry:

What appears to the critic as a contradiction or a discontinuity is merely the attempt by a skillful statesman to try as many approaches as he deems necessary in order to get nearer the very distant goals which his own power position does not allow him to reach directly, easily, or fast. If one approach fails, another will be attempted; often conflicting alternatives are pursued at the same time, both because they point in the same direction in the long run and because if one of them should lead into a dead end he would then still have a number of cards to play.[1]

Thus, de Gaulle initially appeared firm against the rebellion in order both to assure the neutrality of the army while he dismantled key centers of opposition within it to civilian rule (whatever his future policy) and to feel out the position and strength of the FLN (which had now created a Provisional Government of the Algerian Republic, the GPRA). The Constantine Plan for the economic development of Algeria, for example, could be seen either as evidence that France meant to stay permanently in the country (thereby meeting military expectations), or as an attempt to divide the rebellion, or as an indication to the GPRA that it should not ignore the practical benefits to be obtained from cooperation with France.

There were, nonetheless, crucial moments of opposition to de Gaulle's regime from the military-colonial alliance. In January 1960, following his September 1959 offer to the Algerian people of a chance to vote on self-determination, a civilian uprising in Algiers threatened for a few tense hours to gain military support. Again, in April 1961, following de Gaulle's decision to hold a national referendum to approve the creation of a provisional Algerian executive to supervise the forthcoming vote on self-

1. Stanley Hoffmann in his Introduction to Alfred Grosser, *French Foreign Policy under De Gaulle* (Little Brown, New York, 1967), p. viii. A citation from the General's *Mémoires d'espoir* in regard to the Algerian problem illustrates Hoffmann's point: "Il va sans dire que je l'abordais sans avoir un plan rigoureusement préétabli. . . . Mais les grandes lignes étaient arrêtées dans mon esprit . . . faute qu'un courant assez fort porte le pays vers le but et eu égard aux possibilités encore intactes des résistances, je devrai procéder, non point par bonds, mais pas à pas, déclenchant moi-même chaque étape et seulement après l'avoir préparée dans les faits et dans les esprits" (pp. 48, 90).

determination and his recognition of an eventual Algerian Republic, an "Algerian Algeria," four prominent generals sponsored still another uprising against the regime in Algiers. The hesitation of many officers to support it, and the refusal of most conscript troops to obey the generals' orders, sealed the fate of this *Putsch*. Finally, after April 1961, the clandestine Secret Army Organization (OAS), joining civilians and military in Algeria with a heterogeneous assortment of right-wing groups in France, tried to gather the momentum once again to break the authority of the Fifth Republic. But no longer could the myth be propogated that it was the system which was at fault for the loss of Algeria. On the one hand, there was increasing recognition of the strength of nationalist feeling among the Algerian people. On the other, there was the General's reputation and his demonstrated ability firmly to pursue the best interests of France, assuring him a popular legitimacy which the Fourth Republic had come to lack altogether.[2]

In relations with the GPRA, the General had equally complex maneuvers to make. His chief concerns were the future status of the settler community (their civil liberties and property rights), the French role in the Sahara (oil, gas, and atomic test site), France's general reputation within the Third World as a progressive leader (as opposed to the United States), and the good opinion that the French had of themselves in releasing Algeria.

All of these matters would have been settled under terms most favorable to France had the GPRA accepted the conditions the General proposed in his important speech of September 16, 1959. Often this point is missed, since the offer of self-determination and the angry response to it of the military and settlers have apparently misled many to suppose de Gaulle was being far more conciliatory to the rebels than was actually the case. In this address, de Gaulle recognized the right of the Algerian people to decide for themselves on "secession," "association," or "Frenchification." His memoirs attest that the General favored the second solution, believing that secession—a complete break between the two countries—would be a loss for France and a disaster for

2. So low had the legitimacy of the Fourth Republic fallen that in a poll taken in January 1958, only 4 percent of those questioned said they would actively support the Republic against a coup. See Wahl, "The French Political System," p. 207.

Algeria, while discounting Frenchification (another word for the policies earlier discussed as integration or assimilation) as outdated.[3] De Gaulle's option, then, was for what he called association. In his September speech, he declared that in the case of association, "the internal regime of Algeria should be federal, in order that the diverse communities—French, Arab, Kabyle, Mozabite, etc.—which live together in the country, find in it guarantees for their own lives and a framework for their cooperation." Moreover, such a "federal" associated state would have "close union with [France] for the economy, education, defense, and foreign relations." Certainly nothing was novel about this proposition. It shared similarities with both the Declaration of March 24, 1945, Relative to Indochina, and the framework law for Algeria of 1957–1958. Except for the offer of the possible alternative of secession, de Gaulle's proposal differed in no substantial way from Mollet's earlier triptych of cease-fire, elections, negotiations. The General concluded his offer by implying that the GPRA was not representative of the Algerian people, that other political tendencies would have the right to campaign against the GPRA in the forthcoming vote on self-determination, and that this vote might wait for four years after the return of peace to Algeria. However much the speech may have worried the military and settlers, there is no reason to see it as a scheme to grant Algerian independence.

To impress the rebels with the influence he should have in determining the character of an associated Algeria, de Gaulle disposed of two main trumps: the unquestioned military hold of France over the country, and the extreme poverty of the Muslim masses which would require continued and substantial aid from France to survive. On the other hand, as he pointed out in his memoirs, military predominance mattered less as time passed:

3. The speech is reprinted in Charles de Gaulle, *Discours et messages: avec le renouveau, 1958–1962* (Plon, Paris, 1970). Although de Gaulle did not comment negatively on Frenchification for domestic reasons, he did denounce secession in the strongest terms as "leading to a terrible misery, horrible political chaos, generalized throat slitting, and soon a warlike communist dictatorship." A public opinion poll taken five months after the speech, found 6 percent of those interviewed favoring secession, 48 percent favoring association, and 27 percent preferring Frenchification. In other words, the colonial consensus was still very much alive. See *Sondages,* 1960, number 3, p. 55.

France was "sinking politically, financially, and militarily into a bottomless swamp."[4] The demonstrated inflexibility of the GPRA to settle for anything less than full sovereignty, the continued insubordination of the partisans of French Algeria, and his own increasing support from within France decided de Gaulle to make concessions. Thus, on November 4, 1960, fifteen months after his September 1959 address, he recognized that the future Algerian state need not be so limited internally and externally as he had earlier deemed appropriate for association. Still another year was to elapse, however, before (on one occasion after another) he recognized the sovereignty of the future Algerian state over the Sahara, acknowledged the GPRA as the exclusive representative of the Algerian people with whom to negotiate a political settlement of the conflict, and dropped his threats of partitioning Algeria and repatriating the Algerian workers in France.

There may have been some justice to de Gaulle's claim that he was unable to negotiate a settlement earlier with the members of the GPRA, "entangled as they were in their mutual distrust, competition and divisions."[5] But the impasse had to do with the General's own style as well. As he described his initial offer of self-determination: "It is France, eternal France, who alone in her strength, in the name of her principles and following her interests, will accord it to the Algerians."[6] Raymond Aron is perhaps right to criticize the General for his inability to *negotiate* with any of his political adversaries. In the specific case of relations with the leaders of the revolution in 1961, Aron acrimoniously commented, "It is generous France who granted the right to independence; she let nothing be torn from her, she did not lower herself to bargaining."[7] What de Gaulle might have gained by negotiating in earnest sooner than he did is well worth considering (although obviously no final answer is possible), since eventually he conceded every principal demand made by the GPRA.[8]

4. De Gaulle, *Mémoires d'espoir*, p. 49.
5. De Gaulle, *Mémoires d'espoir*, p. 89. On the subject of division within the GPRA, see Quandt, *Revolution and Political Leadership: Algeria, 1954–1968*.
6. De Gaulle, *Mémoires d'espoir*, p. 50. His manner at the time of the Bizerte confrontation with Bourguiba is typical in this regard.
7. Raymond Aron, "Adieu au Gaullisme," *Preuves*, October 1961, p. 5.
8. To take but one important consideration: the OAS did not form until

On the other hand, de Gaulle was as concerned to produce a certain effect on the people of France as to treat with the rebels. In this regard, there is far more to his style than Aron allows when he derides his manner as a "retreat . . . camouflaged under a majestic and thaumaturgic style." For the General realized the importance to France that his policy in Algeria be seen as a victory, if possible, and certainly not as a defeat. As he put it in the summer of 1960: "It is a matter of transforming our old France into a new country and to make her marry her times. It is a matter of drawing prosperity, power, and prestige from this. It is a matter of making this change become our great national ambition."[9] And in the fall of 1961 he renounced colonial empire as "vain and anachronistic, and we no longer believe at all that the interest, the honor, or the future of France is linked, in our period, to the support of her domination over populations who in their great majority do not belong to her population, and which everything leads and will continue to lead to freeing themselves from one another and entering into partnership."[10]

Between 1944 and 1946 de Gaulle had been largely responsible for wedding France to the idea of preserving the empire as a means of keeping rank in the world and healing thereby the wounds of the country's ignominious defeat by Hitler. The tragedy of France (and even more of Indochina and Algeria) was that the inevitable setbacks along this course of redemption only intensified French feelings of national humiliation, driving them all the more not to let the catastrophe of 1940 repeat itself by their fault. They would maintain the empire—or at least Algeria, by far the most important and the most "French" of the colonies—and so live down the curse of division and weakness. It remained for France's master therapist, a man whose genius lay in the manner he persuaded his fellow citizens to think of themselves, to understand the error and to correct it. Once again, as in 1940, Charles de Gaulle had found a reason to declare victory where before his coming the defeat seemed total.

February 1961, in Spain. Had the first Evian meetings of April 1961 brought the settlement which finally came nearly a year later, the OAS would not have had time to insinuate itself into the European community.

9. De Gaulle, *Avec le renouveau,* June 10, 1960.

10. De Gaulle, *Avec le renouveau,* September 5, 1961.

Conclusion

It is commonly observed that politics as an art requires pursuing the desirable in terms of the possible. For this reason, political judgments must be evaluated by their consequences, not by their intentions. The dilemma of leadership is to decide when it is cowardice to fail to exploit the inevitable ambiguities, and therefore possibilities, of the historical moment, and when it is foolhardy to attempt to overcome the immovable constraints set by a combination of forces past and present. Since options are always open to some extent, greatness requires creating opportunities and taking risks within the limits set by history. Yet, all too frequently, political leaders, in their concern for greatness or other values, prove unable to define their policy in terms of the means realistically at their disposal. Instead of political vision informed by rational assessments of difficult situations, policies emerge gilded in rhetoric and counting on gifted improvisation, good fortune, or the ruthless application of force for their success. There are national policies that are evil in themselves. But how much more usually the evil in a policy comes from ignorance of the realities the policy is intended to control and from the efforts that are made to coerce events into the wishful scheme of things toward which the policy is aimed. Such is the story of the policy of the French Fourth Republic toward Algeria and Indochina.

The French ambition after World War II was to retain sovereignty over Algeria. Given the record of French rule for the preceding century in regard to the Muslim population, it is certainly difficult to see how history had established a moral claim on the part of the French to be the political authority there. But there are more practical grounds on which to criticize this ambition: the character of French rule in Algeria combined with developments in international politics to make it highly doubtful that such a claim, legitimate or not, could successfully be pressed long after 1945.

Algeria entered into the struggle to become independent from France not because some mysterious spirit of nationalism swept North Africa, but because 124 years of French rule there had failed to establish the links, either political or economic, which could have integrated the local population with the metropole. To the contrary, the logic of the French presence made such ties virtually impossible to create. As we have seen, French rule in Algeria was characterized by the combination of two lethal elements: a strong settler community and a weak economic structure. The actions of the former shattered Muslim society and held it at bay; the debility of the latter made either the incorporation of the indigenous population into the modern sector, or the separation of the area from France, in the manner of South Africa, an impossible feat. At the same time, Paris was alternately liberal and (more usually) authoritarian in Algeria. It was liberal enough to allow some political mobilization on the part of the Muslims; but having allowed interests to be articulated, Paris silenced them by repression. This contradictory style of rule poorly suited a country with the social and economic characteristics of Algeria: liberality as well as repression prompted the growth of Algerian nationalism.

This does not mean that the rupture between Algeria and France was preordained to occur through revolution. If a series of decisions taken (or not taken) in the first three decades of this century make it doubtful, in retrospect, that, for economic and political reasons, Algeria could be integrated into the Republic, it took only World War II and a combination of other events internal and external to Algeria to bring the area to the point of revolution. For if by 1945, the fact of decolonization was beyond the ability of Paris to control, the specific form that independence would take depended largely on decisions taken in the French capital. Here the formulation and then sabotage of the Statute of Algeria of 1947, along with guarantees to the Muslim population of democratic representation in the National Assembly, were the decisive choices.

But as this text has recounted, policies formulated in regard to Algeria had precious little to do with a realistic assessment of the objective situation there: the Suez invasion of 1956, and the framework law of 1957–1958 are evidence enough of that. Why the situation in Algeria could not be seen realistically, why an orderly transfer of power under conditions favorable to a continued French influence could not be arranged, had to do, to be sure, with the style of the political system in Paris and the genuine interests France had in Algeria. But the key obstacle was the colonial consensus, which understood Algerian nationalism not so much in terms of the evolution of colonial society, but more as a reflection of Anglo-American maneuvers, Communist machinations, and, most basically of all, the incompetent governance of the Fourth Republic. Unable to see the situation for what it was, French action cost the lives of hundreds of thousands of individuals and brought the collapse of the Republic. A regime that is realistic does not necessarily govern well. But a regime that is unrealistic will surely govern ill.

In a library in Paris there is the forgotten journal of an officer who fought with Bugeaud in the first French campaigns in Algeria against the warrior chieftain Abd al-Qadir. After describing the total rout of Berber tribesmen in circumstances that sounded like a massacre, the writer concluded: "We had beaten the British." Over the 110 years separating the final surrender of al-Qadir and the beginning of the Algerian revolution in 1954, this scene was to replay itself in various ways time and again. What Algeria represented to most Frenchmen of all political persuasions had far less to do with the situation in North African than with other concerns, either domestic or international, which had developed for the most part quite independently of what the Third Republic had come to call its three North African departments. One wonders whether the Algerian revolution of 1954, such as it was in leadership, mass following, justification, and promise, ever escaped serious distortion in the eyes of most Frenchmen whom this book has considered, whose hopes and fears made the reality of Algeria as distant as it was for that officer of the 1840's who in killing some poor Berbers thought he was revenging the defeat at Waterloo..

Selected Bibliography

Books

Ageron, Charles Robert. *Les Algériens musulmans et la France, 1871–1919*, 2 vols. Presses Universitaires de France, Paris, 1968.

Ambler, John. *Soldiers against the State*. Anchor, New York, 1968.

Andrews, William. *French Politics and Algeria*. Merideth, New York, 1962.

L'Année politique, économique, sociale et diplomatique. Published annually by Presses Universitaires de France.

Argoud, Antoine. *Le Problème algérien: solution française*. OAS 3ème Section, Bureau d'Etudes, n.d.

Aron, Raymond. *L'Algérie et la République*. Plon, Paris, 1958.

———. *Espoir et peur du siècle*. Calmann-Lévy, Paris, 1957.

———. *Immuable et changeante: de la IVè à la Vè République*. Calmann-Lévy, Paris, 1959.

———. *La Tragédie algérienne*. Plon, Paris, 1957.

Aron, Robert. *Les Origines de la Guerre d'Algérie*. Fayard, Paris, 1962.

Azeau, Henri. *Ho Chi Minh, dernière chance: la conférence franco-vietnamienne de Fontainebleau, juillet 1946*. Flammarion, Paris, 1968.

Barale, Jean. *La Constitution de la IVè République à l'épreuve de la guerre*. Librairie Générale de Droit et de Jurisprudence, Paris, 1963.

Beau de Loménie, Emmanuel. *L'Algérie trahie par l'argent: réponse à M. Raymond Aron*. Editions Etheel, Paris, 1957.

Bloch, Marc. *Strange Defeat*. Norton, New York, 1968.

Bonnafous, Max, ed. *Oeuvres de Jean Jaurès*, Vol. I. Reider, Paris, 1933.

Borella, François. *L'Evolution politique et juridique de l'Union francaise depuis 1946*. Librairie Générale de Droit et de Jurisprudence, Paris, 1958.

Brown, Leon Carl. *State and Society in Independent North Africa*. Middle East Institute, Washington, D.C., 1962.

Brunschwig, Henri. *French Colonialism, 1871–1914: Myths and Realities*. Praeger, New York, 1966.

Camus, Albert. *Actuelles, III: chroniques algériennes*. Gallimard, Paris, 1958.

Cayrol, Roland. *François Mitterrand, 1945–1967.* Fondation Nationale des Sciences Politiques, Paris, 1967.

Chaffard, Georges. *Les Carnets sécrets de la décolonisation,* 2 vols. Calmann-Lévy, Paris, 1967.

Challe, Maurice. *Notre révolte.* Presses de la Cité, Paris, 1968.

Chevallier, Jacques. *Nous, Algériens.* Calmann-Lévy, Paris, 1958.

Clark, Michael. *Algeria in Turmoil: A History of the Rebellion.* Praeger, New York, 1959.

Cole, Allan B. ed. *Conflict in Indo-China and International Repercussions: A Documentary History, 1945–1955.* Cornell University Press, Ithaca, 1956.

Comité Maurice Audin. *Sans commentaire.* Editions de Minuit, Paris, 1960.

Confer, Vincent. *France and Algeria: The Problem of Civil and Political Reform, 1870–1920.* Syracuse University Press, Syracuse, 1966.

Crozier, Michel. *The Bureaucratic Phenomenon.* University of Chicago, Chicago, 1964.

Débatty, André. *Le 13 mai et la presse.* Armand Colin, Paris, 1960.

Demontes, Victor. *L'Algérie agricole.* Librairie Larose, Paris, 1930.

——. *Renseignements sur l'Algérie économique.* Office du Gouvernement Général de l'Algérie, Algiers, 1922.

Déon, Michel. *L'Armée de l'Algérie et la pacification.* Plon, Paris, 1959.

De Porte, Anton W. *De Gaulle's Foreign Policy, 1944–1946.* Harvard University Press, Cambridge, 1968.

Devillers, Philippe. *Histoire du Viet-Nam de 1940 à 1952.* Seuil, Paris, 1952.

Duverger, Maurice, ed. *Partis politiques et classes sociales en France.* Cahiers de la Fondation Nationale des Sciences Politiques, Paris, n.d.

Egrétaud, Marcel. *Réalité de la nation algérienne.* Editions Sociales, Paris, 1961.

Elgey, Georgette. *La République des illusions, 1945–1951.* Fayard, Paris, 1965.

——. *La République des contradictions.* Fayard, Paris, 1967.

Favrod, Charles Henri. *Le FLN et l'Algérie.* Plon, Paris, 1962.

Furniss, Edgar. *France, Troubled Ally.* Harper, New York, 1960.

Gallagher, Charles. *The United States and North Africa.* Harvard University Press, Cambridge, 1963.

Ganiage, Jean. *L'Expansion coloniale de la France sous la Troisième République.* Payot, Paris, 1968.

Gaulle, Charles de. *The Complete War Memoirs of Charles de Gaulle.* Simon and Schuster, New York, 1967.

——. *Discours et messages: pendant la guerre, 1940–1946.* Plon, Paris, 1970.

——. *Discours et messages: dans l'attente, 1946–1958.* Plon, Paris, 1970.

——. *Discours et message: avec le renouveau, 1958–1962.* Plon, Paris, 1970.

——. *La France sera la France.* Bouchy et Fils, Paris, 1951.

——. *Mémoires d'espoir.* Plon, Paris, 1970.

Gettleman, Marvin E., ed. *Vietnam.* Fawcett, New York, 1965.

Girardet, Raoul, et al. *La Crise militaire française, 1945–1962.* Cahiers de la Fondation Nationale des Sciences Politiques, number 123, Paris, 1964.
——. *L'Idée coloniale en France.* La Table Ronde, Paris, 1972.
——. *Pour le tombeau d'un capitaine.* Editions de l'Esprit Nouveau, Paris, 1962.
Gollwitzer, Heinz. *Europe in the Age of Imperialism, 1880–1914.* Harcourt, Brace and World, London, 1969.
Gonidec, Pierre François. *Droit d'outre-mer, I: de l'empire coloniale de la France à la communauté.* Montchrestien, Paris, 1959.
Graham, Bruce. *The French Socialists and Tripartisme, 1944–1947.* Weidenfeld and Nicolson, London, 1965.
Granotier, Bernard. *Les Travailleurs immigrés en France.* Maspero, Paris, 1970.
Grimal, Henri. *La Décolonisation.* Armand Colin, Paris, 1965.
Grosser, Alfred. *La IVè République et sa politique extérieure.* Armand Colin, Paris, 1967.
——. *French Foreign Policy under de Gaulle.* Little Brown, Boston, 1967.
Guérin, Daniel. *Au Service des colonisés, 1930–1953.* Editions de Minuit, Paris, 1954.
Hammer, Ellen. *The Struggle for Indochina, 1940–1955.* Stanford University Press, Stanford, 1967.
Haupt, Georges, and Madeleine Reberioux, eds. *La Deuxième Internationale et l'orient.* Editions Cujas, Paris, 1967.
Heggoy, Alf Andrew. *Insurgency and Counter-Insurgency in Algeria.* University of Indiana Press, Bloomington, 1972.
Hoffmann, Stanley. *Decline or Renewal? France since the 1930's.* Viking, New York, 1974.
Hoffmann, Stanley, et al. *In Search of France.* Harper and Row, New York, 1965.
Humbaraci, Arslan. *Algeria, A Revolution that Failed.* Pall Mall Press, London, 1966.
Isnard, Hildebert. *La Vigne en Algérie,* 2 vols. Editions Ophrys, Gap, 1947.
Jaurès, Jean. *L'Armée nouvelle.* L'Humanité, Paris, 1915.
Julien, Charles André. *L'Afrique du Nord en marche.* Julliard, Paris, 1952.
Kelly, George. *Lost Soldiers.* M.I.T. Press, Cambridge, 1965.
Kolko, Gabriel. *The Politics of War: The World and United States Foreign Policy.* Random House, New York, 1968.
Lancelot, Marie-Thérèse. *Organisation Armée Sécrète,* 2 vols. Fondation Nationale des Sciences Politiques, Paris, 1963.
Lefranc, Georges. *Le Mouvement socialiste sous la Troisième République, 1875–1940.* Payot, Paris, 1963.
Leites, Nathan. *On the Game of Politics in France.* Stanford University Press, Stanford, 1959.
Le Tourneau, Roger. *Evolution politique de l'Afrique du Nord musulmane, 1920–1961.* Armand Colin, Paris, 1962.
Liebesney, Herbert. *The Government of French North Africa.* University of

Pennsylvania Press, Philadelphia, 1943.

Ligou, Daniel. *Histoire du socialisme en France, 1871–1961*. Presses Universitaires de France, Paris, 1962.

Luethy, Herbert, and David Rodnick. *French Motivations in the Suez Crisis.* Mimeo, International Social Research Organization, Princeton, 1956.

Macrae, D. *Parliament, Parties, and Society in France, 1946–1958*. Saint Martin's Press, New York, 1967.

Marshall, D. Bruce. *The French Colonial Myth and Constitution Making in the Fourth Republic.* Yale University Press, New Haven, 1973.

Martin, Claude. *Histoire de l'Algérie française, 1830–1962*. Editions des Quatre Fils Aymon, Paris, 1963.

Massu, Jacques, *Vraie bataille d'Alger*. Plon, Paris, 1971.

Melnik, Constantin. *The French Campaign against the FLN*. Rand Corporation, 1955.

Mendès-France, Pierre. *Gouverner c'est choisir, III: la politique et la vérité.* Julliard, Paris, 1958.

Michel, Andrée. *Les Travailleurs algériens en France.* Centre National de la Recherche Scientifique, Paris, 1955.

Mitterrand, François. *Aux Frontières de l'Union française.* Julliard, Paris, 1953.

——. *Présence française et abandon.* Plon, Paris, 1957.

Mollet, Guy. *Bilan et perspectives socialistes.* Plon, Paris, 1958.

——. *13 mai 1958–13 mai 1962.* Plon, Paris, 1962.

Morgenthau, Ruth S. *Political Parties in French-speaking West Africa.* Oxford University Press, London, 1964.

Naegelen, M. E. *Mission en Algérie.* Flammarion, Paris, 1962.

Nora, Pierre. *Les Français d'Algérie.* Editions de Minuit, Paris, 1960.

Nouschi, André. *La Naissance du nationalisme algérien.* Editions de Minuit, Paris, 1962.

Opperman, Thomas. *Le Problème algérien: données historiques, juridiques, politiques.* Maspero, Paris, 1961.

Passeron, André, ed. *De Gaulle parle.* Plon, Paris, 1962.

Peyerimhoff, Henri de. *Enquête sur les résultats de la colonisation officielle de 1871 à 1895.* Torrent, Algiers, 1906.

Philip, André. *Le Socialisme trahi.* Plon, Paris, 1957.

Pike, Douglas. *Viet Cong: The Organization and Techniques of the National Liberation Front of South Vietnam.* M.I.T. Press, Cambridge, 1969.

Planchais, Jean. *Le Malaise de l'armée.* Plon, Paris, 1958.

Les Procès des Généraux Challe et Zeller. Nouvelles Editions Latines, Paris, 1961.

Le Procès Salan. Nouvelles Editions Latines, Paris, 1962.

Quandt, William. *Revolution and Political Leadership: Algeria, 1954–1968.* M.I.T. Press, Cambridge, 1969.

Rens, Ivo. *L'Assemblée algérienne.* Editions A. Pedone, Paris, 1957.

Roy, Jules. *La Guerre d'Algérie.* Julliard, Paris, 1960.

——. *J'accuse le Général Massu.* Editions de Seuil, Paris, 1972.

Ruedy, John. *Land Policy in Colonial Algeria.* University of California Press, Los Angeles, 1967.

Sartre, Jean-Paul. *Search for a Method.* Knopf, New York, 1963.
——. *Situations,* III. Gallimard, Paris, 1949.
——. *Situations,* V. Gallimard, Paris, 1964.
Savary, Alain. *Nationalisme algérien et grandeur française.* Plon, Paris, 1960.
Servan-Schreiber, Jean-Jacques. *Lieutenant en Algérie.* Julliard, Paris, 1958.
Sivan, Emmanuel. *Communisme et nationalisme en Algérie, 1920–1962.* Presses de la Fondation Nationale des Sciences Politiques, Paris, 1976.
Smith, Tony. *The End of European Empire: Decolonization after World War II.* Heath, Lexington, 1975.
Sorum, Paul C. *Intellectuals and Decolonization in France.* University of North Carolina Press, Durham, 1977.
Soustelle, Jacques. *Aimée et souffrante algérie.* Plon, Paris, 1956.
——. *Le Chemin de la paix.* Centre d'Information pour les Problèmes de l'Algérie et du Sahara, Paris, 1960.
——. *Le Drame algérien et la décadence française: réponse à Raymond Aron.* Plon, Paris, 1957.
——. *L'Espérance trahie.* La Table Ronde, Paris, 1962.
——. *Vingt-huit ans de Gaullisme.* La Table Ronde, Paris, 1968.
Tarr, Francis de. *The French Radical Party from Herriot to Mendès-France.* Oxford University Press, London, 1961.
Thompson, Virginia, and Richard Adloff. *The Malagasy Republic.* Stanford University Press, Stanford, 1965.
Thomson, David, ed. *France: Empire and Republic, 1850–1940: Historical Documents.* Macmillan, London, 1968.
Tillion, Germaine. *L'Algérie en 1957.* Editions de Minuit, Paris, 1957.
——. *Les Ennemis complémentaires.* Editions de Minuit, Paris, 1960.
Varet, Pierre. *Du Concours apporté à la France par ses colonies et pays de protectorat au cours de la Guerre de 1914.* Les Presses Modernes, Paris, 1927.
Weil, Simone. *The Need for Roots.* Putnam, New York, 1952.
Weinstein, Brian. *Eboué. Oxford University Press, New York, 1972.*
Werth, Alexander. *The De Gaulle Revolution.* Hale, London, 1960.
——. *The Strange History of Mendès-France.* Barrie, London, 1957.
Williams, Philip. *Crisis and Compromise: Politics in the Fourth Republic.* Anchor, New York, 1966.
Williams, Philip, and Martin Harrison. *De Gaulle's Republic.* Longmans, London, 1960.
Wright, Gordon. *The Reshaping of French Democracy.* Reynall and Hitchcock, New York, 1948.
Zolberg, Aristide. *One-party Government in the Ivory Coast.* Princeton University Press, Princeton, 1969.

Articles, Reports, Unpublished Material
Ageron, Charles Robert. "Jaurès et les socialistes français devant la question algérienne (de 1895 à 1914)." *Le Mouvement Social,* XLII (January–March 1963).
Aron, Raymond. "Adieu au Gaullisme." *Preuves,* October 1961.

Barbé, Raymond. "Les Classes sociales en Algérie." *Economie et Politique,* September and October 1959.

——. "La Question de la terre en Algérie." *Economie et Politique,* June 1955.

Beloff, Max. "The Special Relationship: An Anglo-American Myth." In Martin Gilbert, ed., *A Century of Conflict, 1850–1950: Essays for A. J. P. Taylor.* Hamish Hamilton, London, 1966.

Berg, Elliott J. "The Economic Basis of Political Choice in French West Africa." *American Political Science Review,* LIV (1960).

Bourdet, Claude. "Y-a-t-il une Gestapo algérienne?" *France-Observateur,* December 6, 1951.

Cassilly, Thomas A. "The Anti-Colonial Tradition in France: The Eighteenth to the Fifth Republic." Doctoral dissertation, 3 vols. Columbia University, 1975.

Duverger, Maurice. "SFIO: mort ou transfiguration?" *Les Temps Modernes,* numbers 112–113.

Girardet, Raoul. "L'Apothéose de la 'plus grande France': l'idée coloniale devant l'opinion française (1930–1935)." *Revue Française de Science Politique,* XVIII (December 1968).

Hoffmann, Stanley. "Les *Mémoires d'espoir.*" *Esprit,* December 1970.

——. "Protest in Modern France." In Morton Kaplan, ed., *The Revolution in World Politics.* Grove Press, New York, 1962.

Isnard, Hildebert, "La Viticulture algérienne: erreur économique?" *Revue Africaine,* Algiers, 1956.

"Monographie du Domaine de la Trappe de Staouéli." *Congrès de la Colonisation Rurale.* Algiers, 1930.

Programme fondamental du Parti Socialiste," *Revue Socialiste,* number 155 (July 1962).

"Rapport générale d'activité." SFIO Party Congresses: 41st (1949), 49th (1957), 50th (1958).

"Sauver l'Afrique française: le dossier du Parti Radical, 1955–1957." Parti Republicain Radical et Radical Socialiste, 1957.

Semedei, Manuela. "L'Empire français à travers les manuels scolaires." *Revue Française de Science Politique,* XVI (February 1966).

——. "Les Socialistes français et le problème colonial entre les deux guerres." *Revue Française de Science Politique,* XVIII (December 1968).

Smith, Tony. "Idealism and People's War: Sartre on Algeria." *Political Theory,* I (November 1973).

Thomas, R. "La Politique socialiste et le problème coloniale de 1905 à 1920." *Revue Française d'Historie d'Outre-Mer,* second trimester, 1960.

Wahl, Nicholas. "The French Political System." In Samuel Beer and Adam Ulam, eds., *Patterns of Government.* Random House, New York, 1962.

Wainwright, William. "De Gaulle and Indochina, 1940–1945." Doctoral dissertation, The Fletcher School of Law and Diplomacy, Tufts University, 1971.

Wall, Irwin. "The French Communists and the Algerian War." *Journal of Contemporary History,* XII (July 1977).

Weiler, Hélène. "Peuplement et démographie." In Jean Alazard et al., *Initiation à l'Algérie.* Maisonneuve, Paris, 1957.

Government Documents

Annuaire statistique de l'Union française. ·Published by the Ministère des Finances and the Ministère de la France d'Outre-Mer.

Annuaire statistique de la zone franc. Published by the Institut National de la Statistique et des Etudes Economiques pour la Metropole et la France d'Outre-Mer.

"Brazzaville: 30 janvier–8 fevrier, 1944." Published by the Ministère des Colonies.

Bulletin mensuel de statistique d'Outre-Mer. Published by the Ministère des Finances et des Affaires Economiques.

Journal officiel. Assemblée Algérienne.

Journal officiel. Assemblée de l'Union Française.

Journal officiel de la République française. Chambre des Députés.

Journal officiel de la République française. Débats parlémentaires, Assemblée Nationale.

Notes et Etudes Documentaires. Published by Service de la Documentation française.

Perspectives décennales de développement économique de l'Algérie. Published by the Ministre de l'Algérie, Algiers, 1958.

Service d'Information du Cabinet du Gouverneur Général de l'Algérie.

Sondages, Revue Française de l'Opinion Publique.

Tableaux de l'économie algérienne. Statistique Générale de l'Algérie, Algiers.

Index

The French Stake in Algeria, 1945–1962

Designed by R. E. Rosenbaum.
Composed by Imperial Litho/Graphics, Inc.,
in 10 point VIP Baskerville, 2 points leaded,
with display lines in Baskerville.
Printed offset by LithoCrafters, Inc.
on Warren's No. 66 text, 50 pound basis.
Bound by LithoCrafters
in Joanna book cloth
and stamped in All Purpose foil.

Library of Congress Cataloging in Publication Data
(For library cataloging purposes only)

Smith, Tony, 1942-
   The French stake in Algeria, 1945–1962.

   Bibliography: p.
   Includes index.
   1. France—Politics and government—1945–1958.   2. France—Politics
and government—1958-   3. France—Colonies.   4. Algeria—History
—Revolution, 1954–1962. I. Title.
DC401.56   944.082   78-7713
ISBN 0-8014-1125-4